S0-BAJ-018

HAGIOGRAPHY OF NARCISA THE BEAUTIFUL

by Mireya Robles

translated by Anna Diegel

with the collaboration of the author

FRANKLIN PIERCE
COLLEGE LIBRARY
RINDGE, N.H. 03461

readers international

The title of this book in Spanish is *Hagiografía de Narcisa la bella*.
Copyright 1985, Ediciones del Norte; 1992, Mireya Robles.

First published in English by Readers International, Inc., USA, and
Readers International, London. Editorial inquiries to RI London office
at 8 Strathray Gardens, London NW3 4NY, UK. US/Canadian inquiries
to RI Book Service, P.O. Box 959, Columbia LA 71418-0959 USA.

English translation Copyright 1996, Readers International Inc.
All rights reserved.

The editors gratefully acknowledge the general support of the National
Endowment for the Arts (Washington DC) as well as specific support
for the translation of this book from the Arts Council of England. The
author also wishes to thank Francesca Lederlin for reading and suggesting
improvements to the English translation.

Cover illustration: Fernando Botero, "Mona Lisa, Age Twelve",
courtesy of the Museum of Modern Art, New York, NY.

Cover design by Jan Brychta.
Printed and bound in the Czech Republic by Ekon, Jihlava.

Library of Congress Catalog Card Number: 96-67376
A catalog record for this book is held by the British Library.

ISBN 1-887378-02-2 Hardcover
ISBN 1-887378-03-0 Paperback

PQ
7390
,R57
H313
1996

NARCISA was born swaddled in a diaper at the edge of the Marsh of Zapata; during Doña Flora's third month of gestation she had sworn to herself that she would clean up her mother's name and coerce her into giving birth, inescapably, within the bounds of legal matrimony; Manengo had been in a hurry and had insisted on being born immediately after Don Pascual had sullied the immaculate honor of Doña Flora; Narcisa the Beautiful knew that she had come into the world to redeem the faults of her fellow men, to conceal them, to inflame the grateful masses, grateful for her virtues, for her perfection, for her conclusive way of shouting that everything was made according to her image and likeness, that she was beautiful and therefore everything was beautiful; and there was Narcisa at the edge of the Marsh, for when she had emerged from Doña Flora's deep canal she had decided that the world did not deserve to see her like that, with such immediacy; with all the placental fluid still slimy around her body she had decided to disintegrate, to evaporate from that bed planted firmly in a room in a house in a street in a block in Baracoa and to fly to the Marsh and meditate on Greek philosophers before allowing the world to lay eyes on her; there, lying on her back in the wet mud, she began imagining the supreme moment when, standing on a platform, she would listen with adoration to her own shouted words: "Republic, Republic, Plato, Aristotle and don't forget Socrates, Krishna, Krishna, Krishna"; those visions rejoiced her small body so much that Narcisa forgot that Doña Flora might desperately be looking for her after noticing that her tunnel was indeed empty and her child born within legal matrimony had not appeared; Narcisa made an effort, she pricked up her ears and caught her mother's voice across the miles separating the two provinces: Pascual, Pascual, where on earth did that boy go? don't tell me I went through this awful birth for nothing, and you, Pascual, what are you waiting for? Don Pascual just remained there, his face wooden and serious as usual, motionless, standing, trying to think up a solution; Narcisa saw him getting worried and his worry gave her a kind of perverse pleasure, for she had clearly heard him say: look Flora, woman, that thing you have in your belly, try to make it a male, for if it's a female I don't even want to see it; on hearing this Narcisa shrank in the womb, experiencing terror for the first time; with her tiny fingers she felt around her groin, a little further in, more to the center, and with despair she confirmed it: there was that tiny slit that Don Pascual seemed to hate her for; every day she made a point of checking and at the hour of her birth the slit was still there, as ineradicable and stubborn as ever, and Narcisa thought of what was to be the first way of playing a trick on her chief enemy, reality; and to cover the slit she provided herself with the diaper in which she was to be born; she was just about to go and meet the people surrounding her mother's bed, but at that moment, with that habit she had of repeating things to herself, she turned on that voice of Don Pascual's she had recorded in her memory: look Flora, try to make this one a real male, because with Manengo you botched it, he's a pansy Flora, a pansy, don't try to tell me he's still a little boy, you can already see what he's coming to; just try to make this one inside you a real male; by dint of willpower Narcisa cut off the voice and concentrated on the job of disintegrating, of moving away, one atom at a time, not forgetting the diaper that covered her; she moved rapidly, in one swoop, and arrived there in time so that Don Pascual was saved from the necessity of doing something; look Flora, there it is, this thing with a diaper on and all; Narcisa longed to return to the hollow her small body had left in the wet mud; she thought it was too early for the struggle which to the end of her life would be signaled by her emphatic gestures and by those shouts of hers that would make the veins of her neck swell; let's see, Pascual, let's see what I just gave birth to, isn't it lovely? for the first time Narcisa heard the foolish laughter followed by crying which later she would so often associate with Doña Flora; she immediately realized that Doña Flora had

3

laughed and cried the way she would whenever something new would come into her hands, first she would praise it automatically, happy with her new possession, without stopping to think whether she liked it or not, without reflecting on what she was seeing, and then she would either decide, yes, how lovely, oh my, yes, how lovely, laughing foolishly and crying again, or she would declare, with her face all twisted: I don't like this, why did I get this if I have no use for it? Narcisa could sense this phrase on Doña Flora's lips, she felt it coming, but the phrase stopped, remained behind Doña Flora's front teeth, adhered to her palate; Don Pascual, with his wooden idol's face, came near the bundle; Narcisa felt his glance gluing itself to her body, weighing down on her neck and she thought, how cruel having to carry this burden so soon; instinctively she tried to defend herself, she drew her legs together, pressed them, clenched them to her small round belly, but Don Pascual separated them with one stroke of his mighty hand; she felt the diaper being wrenched from her and this separation was as painful as if her skin had been torn from her; Don Pascual's glance fell heavily on her tiny sex, searched it slowly, as if time, fragmented into minutes, could have effected a metamorphosis; Don Pascual waited, he waited for an infinitely long time, time became dense, making it impossible for him to escape; for he had dreamed of a son who would bear in straight and round inches that certain extrusion of flesh which tends to symbolize virility; rigid inches which during the hasty formality of proving one's virility would bore deep tunnels into faceless bodies, for faces did not matter, nor did bodies or anything concrete or ethereal either, the main thing was that hasty formality of proving one's virility; and now that object before him, that insignificant opening in an insignificant body which suddenly seemed weary and weak, utterly crushed by a reality it could hide no longer; so Don Pascual wheeled around, turned his back on that object he had placed on the table for closer scrutiny; Doña Flora dared not say anything, she felt no guilt, only a little annoyance at the blank look of near disgust fastened on Don Pascual's face; yet she felt disconcerted by the situation and she only managed to ask: Pascual, Pascual, what shall we name this one? Don Pascual kept moving away without looking at her and he said in a firm resentful voice: Nameless, call her the Nameless One, if you like; Doña Flora thought about this for a while, let a few days pass, finally came to the conclusion that Nameless simply wouldn't do for a newborn girl who had no say in choosing her own name; Doña Flora walked aimlessly around the whole house with a blissful smile on her face, a smile that became a little grotesque when it weighed on the right side of her lower lip, making it hang down; yet she felt excited at the small pleasure of choosing a name without Pascual destroying her illusions, imposing his mother's name or his aunt's or the name of the sister who had died of typhus when he was eleven years old; all those names were rancid, musty, mummified; and Flora thought how awful spending one's life calling by

5

one of those horrible names that bundle which was now lying on its back in the crib Manengo had used before; it was bad enough not to have been allowed to choose her first son's name and she would have had to call him Pascual and feel that hateful name on her lips had not Pancha his godmother nicknamed him Manengo, and because she herself had made it a habit of calling him like that, Pascual had imperceptibly started to use the nickname too; Doña Flora walked to the kitchen sink, she started washing the glasses she had used with Manengo at lunch, with a cloth she scrubbed off bits of orange juice, juice she had made with orange halves pressed over the green glass squeezer, then she washed the deep plates which still contained remnants of red bean soup; absent-minded, she was now washing the flat white plates streaked with egg yolk which had a few grains of rice still left on them; the frying pan and the cast iron pot she would leave for tonight, she was now tired of washing dishes and after all, with that perennial obligation of having to cook for Pascual, everything would get dirty in no time and she'd have to wash dishes all over again; she turned off the tap and dried her hands with her apron while she steered her well-fed body to the kitchen door where she put out her head as if looking for Manengo; what could that boy be up to? she went through the dining room, walked a few steps to the living room and found him naked, seated on the floor, absorbed in the contemplation of some jacks scattered there, which he raised one by one to the level of his eyes with his little left hand and examined fixedly, while his right hand pulled the hanging skin of his small penis; Manengo, Manengo, leave that alone now, that's enough, good heavens you're going to stretch it so much it's going to break some day; Doña Flora could have really gotten mad, she had already been at Manengo a year to make him stop that penis pulling once and for all; last month, during the celebration of his second birthday, at the very instant of putting out the two candles Manengo had decided to tug at his penis, standing there on a chair in front of all the guests who were mainly neighbors and acquaintances from the neighborhood; Doña Flora had lost a little of the composure that she had been saving all along for the time they would get the family picture taken with Don Pascual, with Manengo and with that bulky thing still hiding in her belly; she made her way through the group and cried angrily: naughty, you wretched boy, leave that cursed penis and blow, blow, if you don't do it I'll make you put them out myself; Manengo let go of his hanging bit of flesh, not so much to obey Doña Flora as to let it rest a while, as he had spent the whole day pulling it and it was starting to hurt him a little; Doña Flora felt appeased by what she thought to be obedience and she changed her tone as she addressed her son again, alright my boy, blow, blow; Manengo remained standing on the chair without the slightest intention of blowing, he leaned forward a little to explore with his fingers the blue and white meringue in front of him; look my boy, blow like this, like this; and while demonstrating Doña Flora put out both candles and amidst the neighbors'

7

applause started cutting the cake; Manengo demanded the first piece that was cut from the delicious round mass; Don Pascual seemed to glide among the guests, his face wooden; he barely nodded, assenting with irritation when they said to him, how proud you must be to have a male in the family, look at him over there, how busy he is with that cake, doesn't he look just like a little man when he's eating, I tell you Pascual, that little boy is going to be quite a man; Don Pascual raised the right corner of his upper lip a little in an undecipherable grimace of disgust or exhaustion, moved away from that voice he did not wish to hear and without meaning to, ran into the group of women headed by Flora where the best cake recipes were being exchanged; he arrived there at the very moment when everyone was admiring Flora who had confided to them that the delicious taste of the cake was due to the grated orange rind she had put into it; Don Pascual admitted to himself that he was out of place; he was impatient, this party for Manengo was lasting too long; he felt relieved when the time came for the family picture; the next-door neighbor offered his camera and himself as photographer; Manengo refused to move from where he was seated and Flora and Pascual did what they could to place themselves on the same level as their son; everyone stopped to watch the picture-taking and someone shouted: hug each other and smile; but nobody moved, although they did try to force a smile; Doña Flora leaned over to the floor to pick up the jacks; she had just picked one up when she felt a tug from Manengo and the jack slipped out of her hand; Manengo stretched his legs and stiffened them, as he always did when he was about to fly into a tantrum; Flora saw his small fist clenching, clenching; Flora made a gesture to raise her arm and slap him but she restrained herself, for that incident followed by one of Manengo's lengthy tantrums would have interrupted the process of thinking up a name for the Nameless One; she continued taking a few aimless steps, sat down in a rocking chair, rocked herself a few minutes, made her way to the living room, saw Manengo asleep on the floor, flat on his back, his legs apart like a frog; she thought it might be a good idea to take a little nap herself and after that listen to the three o'clock serial; perhaps some name would occur to her in her sleep; she lay down in her room on the vastness of the double bed, tried to fall asleep and nearly succeeded; the anticipation of the scenes in the serial interrupted her sleep as usual, she wondered if Rosalía del Cueto was really Don Alberto's daughter and if that was the secret she kept, or was it that she carried in her womb Justo Beltrán's child; just think, Rosalía had been on the point of telling the secret that had kept her languishing in bed for such a long time, but the signature tune had interrupted and completely cut off the thread of the story until today at three; when the music started she walked away from the radio to keep herself from giving the announcer a piece of her mind, and although she didn't like talking to announcers, she didn't turn off their voices either, for she understood that this was part of the program: this is CMQ, Partagás, the cigarette that tastes better, Piedra gives you relief; Trinidad y Hermanos, try and compare; Kolonia with a K after your bath; Ironbeer, the refreshment for those who drink with discrimination; Crusellas & Company, always use Hiel de Vaca soap from Crusellas; and after that, music and after the music she did turn off the radio, for the news started and she wasn't interested in that last minute news report stuff; how many times had she told Rosalía del Cueto, alright you little hypocrite, you can tell Don Alberto you don't know Justo Beltrán, but don't give me that rubbish because in last Monday's program he kissed you and you told him very mysteriously and sort of muttering that there was a secret he had to know urgently, but you took such a long time telling him that the organ music got in the middle of it and everybody was left without finding out anything and on top of that you've been lying in bed for a week and you never finish telling anything; and now Justo Beltrán has gone to Chile to work as an engineer in some construction works; the only one left around here is Don Alberto and if you never finish telling anything when are we ever going to find out? could it be that somebody told you that Don Alberto isn't your father? I had already suspected that your Mama was some kind of whore and I know whose daughter you are, as far as I'm concerned you're Ricardo's, he was that traveling salesman for pharmacy supplies, every time he came to town he went to your Mama's house and after they had drunk a cup of coffee in the living room the music started playing and after that all that stuff with

Hiel de Vaca from Crusellas, but I don't miss a thing and all that music was just to cover up your Mama's goings-on; Doña Flora got up all hot and angry with Rosalía; she was used to devoting hours to the solution of these radio problems and she was infinitely thankful to Pascual for giving her free time and for going to the café night after night, or at least that's what he said, and above all for coming home with his underpants full of lipstick, because those whores are really mean, good Lord, they do it just so that us wives will suffer, but they don't know what a favor they are doing me because Pascual could be grabbing women's bottoms at work, I've told him already, look Pascual, it's come to my notice and you'd better look out what you're doing because if you lose that job what are we going to do? but with that cursed man it's hopeless, it's always the same: look Flora my girl, I don't know what you are talking about, and with that same wooden face he always has, out he goes to the café; and if those whores think they're hurting me, well, let me tell you, that really makes me laugh because I just love it, as I said Pascual is grabbing bottoms all day long but when the time comes he can just fire one single shot and if you get it out of him for me, look, I'm happy and more than happy because if there's something that doesn't interest me it's his getting on top of me and go on Flora, open up my girl, how long are you going to keep your legs shut, do you think I'm going to finish this business by magic? and there's no way to get him off me, so I open up and when I see he never finishes the business I start pushing his shoulders to get him down and when I can't any more, I have to tell him, alright Pascual, stop now, how long are you going to keep on? but when you smear his underpants with lipstick I know I won't have to go through the ordeal that night and before going to sleep I can spend an hour or two finding a solution to that business of Rosalía's and practicing what I'm going to tell her in the three o'clock program; Pascual thinks I'm very jealous because when he comes home I inspect his clothes and though I try not to, I can't help saying well, well, these underpants are full of lipstick, and there he stands looking at me with a victorious smile because he thinks I've checked up on his virility and he gets into bed to fill the small space he needs for his body and when I hear him snoring out that rum he's been drinking I ask myself, this dwarf of a man, who does he think he is? Doña Flora looked at the clock and saw it was 2:30 in the afternoon; she was reassured when she saw Manengo still with his legs apart, fast asleep, leaving sweaty spots on the floor; she made her way to the kitchen, got the coffee strainer out of the cabinet to make herself a strong cup of coffee to get rid of her midday drowsiness; she put down the stand, which was made of four small wooden sticks arranged perpendicularly like the edges of a rectangle and held together by a square piece of wood one inch high from the bottom; there you place the pot while the strained coffee drips; on the upper part, the sticks are joined together by another square of wood in the center of which there is a round hole; this is where you place the cloth filter held by a wire hoop in which you put in the ground coffee; Doña Flora was generous and put in several spoonfuls of coffee and several more of sugar while the water was heating on the masonry coal range; when she heard the water bubble she poured it into the filter and waited for it to fill the enamel pot; she got her cup out, filled it to the brim and went to sit down in the rocking chair to enjoy it at her leisure and to go for the last time over the sentences with which she was going to confront Rosalía del Cueto, to begin with, if I had been your mother I wouldn't have given you this name, imagine naming you Rosalía, that's the limit, calling you just the same as that Rosalía Martínez who irritated me so much at the little day school in the country when I lived at my father's farm, alright, and you Rosalía Martínez, why do you laugh at my Papa and at my family and at the farm? if we didn't get more out of the farm that was because the ground was full of stones and nobody can do anything about that, we might have been poor but laughing at us like that is disgraceful and just because your Papa is a landowner, that doesn't give you the right to call my Papa a good-for-nothing, look, if I don't tell you what you deserve it's because I don't want to get into trouble, there is decency in silence, but when I'm at the farm and I remember you I say, you good-for-nothing, that's what you are, a good-for-nothing; and now it looks like you too got to be called Rosalía, alright, it wasn't you who chose it, it must have been Don Alberto or that whore of a mother of yours or maybe Ricardo, but it would have been better if they had named you Narcisa, she's that woman who falls in love with water and right she is to fall in love because Pascual who's always working in the offices of the Health Department knows the importance of water and aqueducts, that's why you could have called yourself lucky, Rosalía del Cueto, if they had named you Narcisa; after the last sip of coffee Doña Flora saw by chance that the dial of the living room clock indicated 3:05; she wanted to check what Manengo was doing: she saw him lying on his back, holding a soft rubber ball in his hands, spinning it, making it turn between his fingers and looking at it attentively; she got up without making a noise and quickly went to pour herself another cup of coffee; she was worried about the serial, she was sure that Rosalía had told the secret and that she had missed it all after waiting so long, but to her relief she realized that she had not missed anything: Rosalía was still lying in bed and did not want to talk, and Toya, the black servant who had been present at her birth, now brought her a cup of linden tea to soothe a pain and suffering whose origin no one could yet imagine; the program went on without any important scenes and perhaps for this reason Doña Flora restrained herself from arguing with the characters, but also perhaps because she had other things on her mind, like that problem of finding a name, for after all, if she had the authority to choose and didn't choose, what right did she have to be given such an opportunity? after the music, Hiel de Vaca from Crusellas and Kolonia with a K, she turned off the radio and remained deep in thought, as if

14

meditating profoundly; she gradually returned to reality, remembering it was time for Manengo's bath; she was sorry to get up from the chair without having found a solution; however, as she raised her sweaty buttocks from the straw chair she felt the whole house was illuminated with the enormous and perfect name of NARCISA; she made her way to the crib, there lay that thing with her round eyes fixed on the ceiling, scarcely moving, her diapers wet with all the urine that Doña Flora had let accumulate, not because she did not care, but because she had had to attend to other things like watching Manengo and finding solutions to that business of Rosalía del Cueto's; Doña Flora leaned over the crib a little and she said with an expression of near triumph: Narcisa, you are Narcisa; the small bundle remained motionless but for the first time it smiled a little to show that it approved of its name; Doña Flora looked over that object she had just saved from being the Nameless One for ever, she noticed the wet diaper, resigned herself to changing it, unfastened the safety pins and when she opened the front of the diaper she saw the swollen lips eaten by a rash and wondered at Narcisa having spent so much time without crying; she ran a moist antiseptic cloth between her legs, she applied vaseline and went to the chest of drawers to get the talcum powder but she thought that at this stage talcum powder would only irritate her more and she set out to change the diaper; months followed without her being able to find out what Rosalía's secret had been, for she had shouted at her so much at the moment when

Rosalía had been about to reveal it that she had frightened Manengo out of his sleep and he had flown into a tantrum and so if she hadn't shouted at Rosalía, tell us, finish telling us, I know who you are anyway, Rosalía would have told the secret and she could have heard it; Doña Flora felt cheated because Don Alberto and Toya and all the servants and all their friends were attending Rosalía's and Justo Beltrán's happy wedding, the honeymoon was already arranged, they were going to Chile where Justo would carry on being an engineer, and to think that they all knew the secret she had lost with her imprudence, but that's life, alright, better luck with the next soap, *The Victim Unforgiven*, right now I have to think about how we are going to celebrate Narcisa's birthday, it's just around the corner; I don't feel like making a cake or doing too much work, so Pancha can just make ice cream in her churn as she said she would, but people talk for the sake of talking and promise a lot and afterwards they give you nothing, we'll see what Pancha comes up with; that Friday afternoon Don Pascual arrived earlier than usual, Flora got up reluctantly from the rocking chair to give him clean underpants and an undershirt, a towel and soap, in other words to prepare Don Pascual's bath as she did every day; Don Pascual had arrived looking more serious than usual, he addressed his wife rudely, well, I imagine Martinita, Armando Brito's wife, has told you already, hasn't she? Doña Flora looked at him, trying to understand, until her husband explained, well, it's just that Armando insists that we spend a couple of days at

16

his beach house over in Maisí, but I explained I had an engagement Saturday and Sunday and I was sure you wouldn't want to go; Doña Flora laughed in the same foolish way she did whenever she received presents, then she started crying, of course I want to go, Pascual, why shouldn't I want to go? just imagine, swimming in the sea with Manengo and spending a few days at the beach, what a dream, when are we going? Don Pascual could not conceal a shrug of disapproval as he answered, tonight Armando's brother-in-law is coming to get us in the jeep, we can come back with him on Sunday, Armando and his wife are going to be in Santiago for the week-end; Doña Flora transmitted her enthusiasm to Manengo who let himself be bathed, clothed and sprinkled with talcum powder without offering any resistance; she filled two old traveling bags with clothes and two straw shopping bags with fruit and things to eat, for Armando had not said that food was included in the invitation; she went over to Narcisa's room and she started to take diapers out of a chest of drawers, she stopped and looked at the bundle with an expression that Narcisa could read very clearly: why did I get this if I didn't want it? but the words adhered to the arch of her mouth and Narcisa understood without having to hear any words; while she was arranging the diapers, Doña Flora felt a childish joy at the thought of what Manengo would do in the water and Narcisa did hear these words spoken aloud: how Manengo will enjoy it, I'd love to see him in the water; while she was leaning over the shopping bag, Doña Flora was startled

17

by the unexpected sound of a loud and powerful groan coming from Narcisa's crib; after regaining her composure a little she drew near and saw a black filament oozing out of the left corner of her lips, streaking across the face and ear like a thin petroleum snake; Doña Flora quickly cleaned it up with toilet paper which she threw into the wastepaper basket; she finished filling the shopping bag and brought it to the living room; Don Pascual came over in his bath slippers, undershirt and underpants: I'm through with my bath, why don't you take one so you can start serving the meal, I'm hungry; listen, what's that funny face you're making now? don't you want to go to the beach? well, if that's what you want, let's go then; Doña Flora remained looking fixedly at an undefined point, I don't know, Pascual, all we need now is something to happen that keeps us from going, that's all we need; Don Pascual looked at her wearily, that's enough of that, woman, that's enough, get done with your bath; Doña Flora vanished into the bedroom and returned in a bathrobe, with a towel in one hand and in the other a bottle of Kolonia with a K; after her bath Doña Flora, still in her bathrobe, served the meal: meat stuffed with ham, cassava with *mojo* dressing, red beans and rice, fried plantains; Manengo demanded to be given the first plate; Pascual consented, for demanding like that was a virile thing and a quality he would never think of discouraging in his male child; Doña Flora opened the door of the small ice-box, looked at what was there and then, listen Pascual, what kind of beer do you want, a

18

Cristal or a Hatuey? I've told you already, the one I like is Polar, who told you to buy brands I didn't ask for? well, listen, what do you want me to do, the man at the food shop on the corner told me he didn't have any more Polar, so do you want a beer or not? Don Pascual looked at her as if to give her the correction she deserved, but he was hungry and he did not want to delay the supper with a fight; give me the Hatuey; with some annoyance he saw Flora place a Cristal in front of her glass, that's just what I need, that she should take my beer; the first bite of meat seemed delicious to him but it did not occur to him to compliment Flora, does she think that because her Mama was born in Mantilla near Havana and because she inherited that way of calling *guineos* "plátanos manzanos" from her mother and says the "food shop" on the corner instead of the grocery store, does she think that gives her the right to fly at me if I want a Polar? who does she think she is, a general? just as he was about to finish Don Pascual realized that because of her he had not been able to enjoy the meal and he decided to concentrate on dessert, guava halves in syrup with cream cheese followed by freshly made coffee, but as he was eating the second piece he raised his fork and pointed it at Doña Flora: if you cooked like that every day it would be a pleasure to eat in this house, but when do you ever come up with anything nice? Doña Flora felt encouraged by the beer and she jumped at him, alright, with that measly salary you're bringing home, do you think we have enough for anything? if we eat like this today it's because you've

19

just gotten paid, but the other days, with the little you earn and with what you spend on that lipstick on your underpants, alright, tell me how can it ever be enough! okay Flora, if you don't like it, what can I do? do you want me to become a queer? and saying this he looked at Manengo who at that moment had left fork and knife on his plate and looked at him unflinchingly, challenging him; at about nine o'clock that night Luis, Armando's brother-in-law arrived; Doña Flora had just finished washing the dishes and had made two sandwiches with the left-over meat; Luis helped them with the parcels, Doña Flora suggested, you Pascual, take care of Narcisa and I'll take Manengo and one of the shopping bags; Don Pascual made a noticeable grimace before exclaiming, no, you can take that one yourself; Doña Flora carried the Nameless One all wrapped up like one of those dummies used in the movies to represent babies; she thought she would put her on the front seat, close to herself, the place she usually chose on the few times they rode in a car, but Manengo demanded to go in front too, and so the bundle was placed on the back seat with Pascual; the movement of the car, the meal and the beer were making Pascual sleepy, and to be more comfortable he pushed the bundle further and further into the corner and fell asleep; Narcisa felt smothered by her father's weight and the suffocation became almost painful, but she did not protest; she fixed her eyes on the canvas ceiling and waited for the trip to end; Manengo's first contact with the beach was pleasant; he sat down at the water's edge, getting his feet wet; he wore a red woolen bathing suit with a white canvas belt; Doña Flora wore her black woolen suit, which emphasized her enormous white body; in his black woolen trunks Don Pascual seemed prematurely flabby, especially in that flesh under the nipples; his body contrasted with his sustained firm gaze of a silent titan; Don Pascual steered his small steady frame towards the sea; walking near Doña Flora who was still sitting on the sand he asked her listlessly and without expecting an answer, hey Flora, aren't you going for a dip? Doña Flora did not alter her smile of enjoyment, caused by the combination of sand and sun and by the proximity of the sea and she answered without thinking of what she was saying: yes, in a little while, in a little while I am going for a dip; Don Pascual walked over to the shore towards Manengo; without a word he got into the water to show him how to swim; or to show him, more than anything else, that he, Don Pascual, could swim; Manengo was amusing himself with three shells he had just collected and was paying no attention to Don Pascual's swimming and diving; when Don Pascual finally became tired of trying to impress him, he decided to come out of the water and to go near Manengo once more; look my boy, come here, come to your Papa, I'll show you how to dive like a man, come on, give me your hand and walk with me; Manengo gave his father his hand and stood up, not because he had the slightest intention of letting himself be ducked, but because he wanted to get into the water a bit and was afraid of going alone; when Doña Flora saw her son with Don Pascual she walked towards them, forgetting the bundle she had left on the shore; when she came near them she burst into that foolish laughter she uttered sporadically, that laughter followed by crying and with what seemed genuine emotion she remarked while she looked at them: how nice this boy looks, how nice he looks with his Papa; when she finished that sentence Manengo had already walked in knee-deep and refused to go any further; when Don Pascual tried to pick him up in his arms Manengo freed himself in one jolt, clutched his penis with his right hand and stiffened his legs as if about to fly into a tantrum; Don Pascual moved his head without trying to hold Manengo, looked in front of him and was grateful to see Flora there and to be able to let off steam at somebody, see, it's useless, this boy doesn't like anything men like; Doña Flora made no comment, for she was not going to ruin what promised to be a lovely morning; she took a few steps, walked into the water and gave herself a hip bath; she had been enjoying the water for some time when she noticed that the few people who remained in the water were rapidly swimming to shore, especially those on her right, about five hundred meters away; a boy of about fourteen ran past her, she stopped him by shouting: what's going on? why are people running? the boy, slender and light, stopped a few seconds, it's nothing lady, it stinks of rotten eggs and the sea is getting black over there, it all comes from that dead thing, that dead animal with a swollen belly you see floating over there; suddenly

Flora remembered the bundle she had left on the shore and she gave a start on noticing it was not there; she remembered that at the very moment she had been complimenting Manengo, how nice this boy looks, how nice he looks with his Papa, she thought she had heard a hoarse moan which she had recognized as Narcisa's, at the time she had not wanted to stop or leave the wonderful sight of the boy with his Papa, but now it was impossible to ignore this; she had to leave her bath and she started walking, dripping with water, Pascual, Pascual, Narcisa isn't there, Narcisa has disappeared, let's go find her, where is she? where could she be? Don Pascual stopped his wife, seizing her firmly by the arm, there she is, floating in the water, what's gotten into her to start floating in the sea? Doña Flora accelerated the movement of her bulk, but good Lord, Pascual, do something, don't just stand there, do something; there's nothing I can do, Flora, that one won't go away so easily, you can be sure she'll come back on her own and in a minute she'll be back with us; the people were dispersing and the beach remained empty even after the water had become clear again; Don Pascual went on diving, Doña Flora remained on the sand and fanned herself with a cardboard fan with a wooden handle that had a picture of Betty Grable in front and an advertisement for La Comercial, "the people's store," on the back; Manengo kept sitting on the shore, his body half immersed in the water, examining the same shells; Don Pascual stood up decidedly, gave a few slaps on the water as if to take leave of it, wiped the water from his face with his hands and walked over to the shore, listen Flora, how long are we going to stand here with this? I'm hungry and I can't wait any more, it's three o'clock and we haven't had lunch yet, look, don't tell me that stuff about fruit and sandwiches, for me if it's not a hot meal it's no meal at all, you can stay here if you want to, but I'm going to eat at the Ranchón, it's well past lunch time; Doña Flora stopped the fan's motion, got up helping herself with her hands, called Manengo who did not move until he saw his parents walking away and then started running to follow them; at the Ranchón Don Pascual, not consulting his wife, ordered from a menu sticky with grease, alright, bring us an order for two, crab *enchilados* and boiled yams and a Polar beer for me and two glasses of water; Doña Flora quickly added, waiter, a Hatuey for me, nice and cool; Manengo, striking the table with his small fist, also demanded: Coca Cola! without consulting Don Pascual the waiter added one Hatuey, one Coca Cola to the order; the *enchilados* were cooked in beer, with tomato sauce, garlic, onion and Spanish oil and were delicious; after lunch Don Pascual insisted on going to the beach house and taking a nap, that second Polar had made him drowsy in the afternoon heat; Doña Flora wanted to suggest something to him, but all she did was follow him, holding Manengo's hand; once there, everyone settled down to sleep; Don Pascual and his wife on the double bed in the main bedroom; Manengo on a canvas cot in the living room; they took a long deep nap and Doña Flora was the first to wake up, with a little start;

24

she raised her hand to her breast to wipe her sweat with the cloth of her dress; she sat up on the bed and dried her forehead with the handkerchief she had left on the bedside table; she looked at Don Pascual, wishing she could wake him by an act of willpower, but Don Pascual kept on sleeping; she heard Manengo walking around the house, she saw him coming rapidly towards Don Pascual like a small bull about to charge; Doña Flora did not stop him, she saw him raise his small fist and give a punch in her husband's soft stomach while crying out in a commanding voice: Coca Cola! Don Pascual jumped up and opened his eyes, not entirely understanding what had happened; Doña Flora gave him no time to analyze the situation; before her husband could become furious she spoke quickly, Lord, Pascual, it's just as well you woke up, we'd better hurry before it gets dark, remember we have to go back to the beach; Don Pascual ignored the punch, yawned and ordered his wife to get his bath ready, he felt uncomfortable with all that salt sticking to his body and he wasn't going to go out anywhere without taking a bath first and they should do the same, she and Manengo, for if salt remains on your body too long it can be bad for you; Doña Flora did not dare protest for fear that her husband would refuse to go back to the beach; she ran the bath and when he had finished and was getting dressed she bathed Manengo and dressed him and poured a little Kolonia with a K on him, finally she took a quick bath herself, put on a sleeveless cotton dress, a light blue one with dark blue flowers, and took Manengo's hand so

25

that her husband would understand it was time to go; Don Pascual finished adjusting his suspenders and followed his wife reluctantly; when they came to the shore it was nearly evening and a bluish shadow was spreading over the sand; the three of them were walking, trying not to get their shoes too wet; Don Pascual walked in an easy fashion, swinging Manengo's small hand in his own and Manengo submitted to this intimacy with his father, for he did not like the near-darkness and the emptiness of the beach; Doña Flora walked ahead, looking at the ground, searching, searching attentively until she could make out the outline of the bundle made of flesh and cloth; she gathered it up in her arms, uncovered Narcisa's face and said with a certain tenderness which Narcisa was receiving from her mother for the first time, good Lord, my child, what a mess you look; Narcisa could not bear such a sentimental moment without taking a deep breath, as though she were about to sob, but she was cut short by her mother's imperious voice: look Pascual, let's turn back, now that everything is settled all I want to do is get home quickly and change, because this bundle's got me all soaked; when they came home Pascual rushed in to listen to the radio and hear the results of the afternoon's game; he was a fan of the Almendares and the waiter had told him the team from Cienfuegos was winning; Doña Flora resigned herself to not being able to listen to any radio program, they were not as good as the serials but they usually entertained her; Manengo sat in the living room near his

Papa, but aloof, still absorbed in the contemplation of the shells he had collected on the beach; Doña Flora was now feeling more comfortable in a dry and fresh piqué housedress; she lay back on the bed to thumb through *Vanidades* magazine, hoping she would find news of her favorite stars, but there was nothing there, not a single word about Olga Chorens or Toña la Negra or Otto Sirgo, alright, it seemed today wasn't her day for fun and she resigned herself to getting things ready for the return trip; Luis had arranged to pick them up on Sunday morning at eleven, and I'd better get everything ready tonight for tomorrow so we can sleep late in the morning; Doña Flora filled both traveling bags and one of the straw bags, the other was to be used for the clothes they had worn at the beach during the day and that she had hung out to air a little on the clothes-line in the patio; after doing the chores she settled down to sleep, her mind at ease after seeing that Don Pascual looked tired after the day at the beach and seemed to have no intention of bothering her that night; before lying down Doña Flora took off Manengo's clothes, for he was starting to rub his eyes sleepily and she laid him down on a single bed in a separate room adjoining their bedroom; she fell fast asleep and did not notice Don Pascual taking off his shoes, his socks, his suspenders, his pants, his shirt, his undershirt and remaining in his underpants to get more air from the small fan in the bedroom; he left all his clothes scattered about the floor, climbed under the mosquito net and without looking at his wife, fell asleep on his left side; at nine in the morning Doña Flora was up and she filtered coffee to prepare the *café con leche* with the liter of milk the waiter from the Ranchón had left her in the morning after she had ordered it and which he had brought together with a *flauta* of bread and some butter; Doña Flora had thought of giving the waiter a *medio* as a tip, but later she thought her husband might complain if he got wind of it and she wasn't going to let anyone annoy her and besides, he's getting paid for being a waiter and surely also for running errands; Manengo appeared in the kitchen as if he had guessed the *café con leche* was ready and the buttered bread all cut and served on a plate on the dining room table; he sat down at the table naked as he was and started eating the bread dipped in milk, swallowing large pieces swelled with hot liquid; Don Pascual came out of the bath and started to eat, not even saying good morning; when it was Doña Flora's turn there was not much bread left, but she could at least fill her large cup to the brim with milk; she tried to wash the dishes quickly so Don Pascual would not start shouting if Luis arrived and she was not ready; she picked up the two mosquito nets, the one on the big bed and the one on the small bed where Manengo had slept; she made the bed, swept up the sand they had left on the floor and sat down on the sofa in the living room to wait for Luis; it was then that she saw on the canvas cot the bundle still in its damp clothes, just as she had left it the night before; she resigned herself to removing all the wet clothing, ran a moist cloth over the body and changed the diaper; then she remembered there was no

28

milk left, and even if there had been any she would not have had time to warm it up and start washing up again; Narcisa would eat when they got to Baracoa; the week passed without major events, except for the delay in broadcasting *The Victim Unforgiven;* they keep announcing it but they don't broadcast it because of some problem at the radio station; at three o'clock in the afternoon as usual, Doña Flora heard the substitute program without the slightest enthusiasm, for the truth was, it wasn't anything anybody could get excited about; and yet, something had happened that week which in a certain way had made her happy: at three o'clock in the afternoon, while she was glued to the radio, Manengo went to Narcisa's room and remained there during the whole half hour of the program; Doña Flora felt more relieved than ever, for in fact she had sometimes told herself that perhaps she ought to pay a little more attention to her daughter; but on the other hand, she was leading a normal Mama's life: she cooked, she looked after the house, she took care of Manengo and Pascual and she even sacrificed herself when Pascual took it into his head to get on top of her, but it wouldn't be a bad idea if someone, even only Manengo, would pay a bit of attention to Narcisa; Manengo went stealthily into the room and locked the door; he stood next to Narcisa's crib as he had been doing for days; he pulled down his shorts and was left naked; with his right hand he started tugging his penis and he repeated like a litany, take it off, take it off, take it off; fifteen ritual minutes had passed, which Manengo had learned to calculate, mastering the mystery of the passage of time; at the appointed moment he let go of the penis and moved towards Narcisa who was ready, her legs open, without a diaper; Manengo squeezed the lips of the small sex in his fist and repeated another litany: mine, mine, mine; at the appointed time he pulled up his shorts, put Narcisa's diaper back on, left the room and sat down on the living room floor to play with paper dolls; Narcisa remained in the near-obscurity of the closed room, her round sienna colored eyes looking at the ceiling; she had been deeply moved by her brother's presence and by this new experience in her life; she swore to herself that she would carry out an eternal pact with Manengo, that she would understand him better than anybody, that she would share his feelings; nobody until now had understood him, nobody had seen the necessity for that obsession of his to tear off a sex he did not like, a sex which was not in harmony with his delicate and meditative spirit; although she was not too sure whether she should believe in the effectiveness of her brother's ritual, it might succeed yet, for her brother was a powerful being and if it did, once in possession of her brother's sex she would emerge from her limitations and from her obscurity and strive towards light and recognition; if everything came out wrong and the change did not take place, her brother would at least remember that she had tried to be his ally and from now on he would not ignore her as completely as he had before; during her hours of profound meditation Narcisa remembered what pains

30

her mother took so that people would compliment her daughter; she would tie a yellow ribbon in her sparse coarse hair and she would go out on the street pushing the baby carriage, walking at the pace Manengo had chosen; fortunately he usually preferred to walk slowly, his arms crossed behind him, looking at the ground as if trying to decipher some mystery hidden in the pavement; and so they walked through town and when Doña Flora met one of her friends and tried to wrest a few words of praise out of her for Narcisa, it was always the same, the compliment was for Manengo; sometimes Doña Flora dared insist, look at the girl, isn't she pretty? but she never received an answer; when Doña Flora came home she unburdened her mind to Pascual, repeating the eternal complaint: today it was the same, Pascual, the same thing as ever, nobody said a word to her; okay Flora, what does it matter whether they say anything or not? good Lord, Pascual, how is it not going to matter, do you know what it is to have a daughter and nobody pays her any compliments? do you know how bad I feel every time Teresita tells me she had to buy an *azabache* for her daughter because people complimented her so much that she felt she had to protect her against the evil eye? and it's the truth, because the girl always has an *azabache* pinned to her dress; do you know what it means to me, Pascual, not being able to tell anybody I had to buy an *azabache*? Narcisa felt deeply ashamed when she remembered all this, but she told herself that perhaps all these miserable experiences were reaching an end and that meanwhile her brother

31

needed her; there he was, day after day, trying to snatch her sex and giving her the hope that thanks to his magic she might succeed in becoming the man of the house; and in the name of their newly discovered solidarity she decided to clutch the bars of the crib and stand up on the mattress that was her floor; Doña Flora was sitting on the rocking chair, freshly bathed and waiting for her husband, with the meal ready to serve when Pascual would come out of the bath; that evening during the meal she would speak to him about the birthday and she did just that; she served Don Pascual a plate of rice and chicken, left-overs from yesterday's chicken: neck, liver, gizzard, the heart and a leg which Manengo started to eat; Pascual enjoyed the rice but he did not like having so little meat, though he did not say anything, for he realized that his wife was in no mood to tolerate complaints; he just carried on eating the rice, the lettuce and tomato salad and the fried green plantains which he found very tasty; Doña Flora waited until dessert, her husband was enjoying a dish of large mangoes her friend Pancha had brought her that afternoon, sharing the sack of mangoes from the trees that grew on her brother-in-law's farm and which he had given to her; Don Pascual looked at the dish, studied the size of each mango and chose the largest; after he had devoted some time to sucking on the stone with the greatest enjoyment Doña Flora took advantage of the opportunity: listen Pascual, in a few days it's going to be Narcisa's birthday, don't you think we should celebrate it? what do you think we should do? Don Pascual took the mango out of his mouth and without attaching any importance to the question, what do you mean Flora, what should we do? you don't think Narcisa is going to understand anything about birthday celebrations at one year of age, do you? Doña Flora opened her mouth to remind him that they had always celebrated Manengo's birthday, including his first one, but she realized that her husband was in no mood to turn his attention away from the task of eating mangoes to worry about Narcisa's birthday; after the meal Doña Flora let her husband listen to the news without expressing any protest; and now, under the mosquito net, Doña Flora renewed the conversation: look Pascual, I don't think it's fair to celebrate Manengo's birthday and not the girl's; and what's more, if we don't do it, what are the neighbors going to say, that we don't care for our daughter? Don Pascual turned over on his left side, refusing to listen to any more of his wife's chatter; Doña Flora insisted once more: look Pascual, this is the limit really, the girl is going to be one year old and we haven't even baptized her, just imagine what an embarrassment now that I've started going to mass every Sunday, you surely realize that all the women in the neighborhood go to mass and what a shame it would be if I didn't go too and you can't tell me we've had to make any expenses for that, not even for the mantilla, I wear the one I inherited from my mother and for clothes, well, I manage as I can and if I can't go around in new clothes like all the others, well, I go without new clothes, it's not the first time, but don't you think it's time we got Narcisa baptized? honestly, I

33

don't know what to say to Pancha, to Martinita, to Teresita and to all the others, it's getting embarrassing, everybody who is anybody gets his children baptized; you're the only one who doesn't pay attention to such things; Don Pascual had to make an effort to endure this voice which did not let him go to sleep; he consented, above all so that she would be silent, okay, get her baptized, but forget about that birthday celebration, we'll have enough expenses with the priest, good night now, that's enough, Flora, good night; Flora was happy with the new prospect of having her two children baptized as it is done in decent families; during the following days she took it upon herself to speak to Father Alvarez and arrange a date for the christening, which would take place on the following Sunday at nine o'clock in the morning; Martinita and Armando Brito would be godparents and would give the girl the christening gown, in this way they wouldn't have to make the expense; Doña Flora went to Narcisa's room to give her the news of her christening and she was astonished to see her standing up, clutching the bars of the crib, rigid, like a soldier at attention; Doña Flora was also surprised to see that Narcisa seemed on the watch, attentive, as if waiting for a piece of news: look Narcisa, in a few days we're going to take you to church and get you baptized; Doña Flora was not quite sure, but it seemed to her that Narcisa was moving her head as a sign of approval, this was a lot more than she had expected, the main reason why she had gone to speak to Narcisa was that she needed to tell somebody the news, but never had she dreamed of getting the slightest reaction from that bundle of flesh; the same afternoon Martinita brought the white batiste christening gown trimmed with pink satin ribbons at the shoulders; Flora burst into her little laughter followed by tears, she was thrilled with the dress, which at that moment she was not really connecting with Narcisa; Manengo had taken no interest in the preparations for the christening until now, but when he saw the gown he wished somebody would put it on him, he wanted to feel the ribbons protecting his shoulders with that pink color he liked so much; Manengo felt an annoyance he could not master, for he knew that there was no question of demanding his rights with a punch and that he had no power to take possession of the christening gown; after the christening Doña Flora was thinking of offering white bread sandwiches, slices cut into four small triangles, for the idea wasn't to fill people up but just to show them a little courtesy; and if her brother Beto brought her the sour-sops he had promised her, that would be enough, with them she'd make a punch to serve with the sandwiches and that would do; as a filling she had thought of a few cans of deviled ham mixed with cream cheese and an eighth of a pound of butter; as soon as Martinita had gone after drinking a cup of freshly made coffee, she placed the christening gown on the sofa and looked at it for a long time; she had to admit that Martinita and Armando had given her a nice present; she sat down in a rocking chair in front of the sofa, slowly sipping another cup of coffee while she admired

35

the fine batiste cloth, the hem stitch, the tiny pleats, the shiny pink satin; she lost the notion of time; after a while she decided to get up; she turned her glance away from the sofa and met Manengo's strange fixed stare; without knowing why, at that precise moment she connected the christening gown with Narcisa, she ought to try it on her, it looked as though it would fit her nicely, but why run the risk? suppose the day of the christening she discovered it didn't fit? she made an effort and decided to go up to Narcisa's room, the only room that was upstairs; the movement of her body being pulled up the stairs felt uncomfortable to her; when she was upstairs she turned to the right; she took a few steps along the little hallway; she opened the door of the room on her left, she entered the semi-darkness that filled the room even in the morning because of the lack of windows; there she faced Narcisa who was standing up in the crib, clutching the bars, at attention and wearing a smile of approval that startled her mother; for a while Doña Flora looked at the round eyes, at the sparse coarse hair, at that curious shape of Narcisa's mouth and nose which bulged out and flattened up in front and for the first time Doña Flora was able to associate these protuberances with an image that came into her mind: the image of the Chinese dragons she had seen in some magazine pictures, pictures which she invariably avoided, thumbing quickly through the pages in order to pass over them; Doña Flora went up to her daughter, who was naked except for a diaper; she wiped her body with a moist cloth to remove the dirt that might soil the christening gown, and she resigned herself to changing the diaper so that the batiste would not become impregnated with the smell of urine; while changing the diaper Doña Flora tried to lay Narcisa down, but she felt a certain resistance which she did not feel like struggling with at that moment and so she changed her standing up; when she put the gown over her head Doña Flora noticed her daughter's cooperation, Narcisa hastened to put her arms into the sleeves and remained still so that her mother could fasten the small mother-of-pearl buttons that made a line down the back; after being dressed Narcisa clutched the bars firmly and looked fixedly at her mother, seeking her approval; Doña Flora felt a little breathless when she saw that the delicate dress did not change the dragon features; she was dismayed at the lack of harmony in the sight before her and she thought she had better get used to the fact that nobody was going to pay any compliments to the bundle on the christening day, unless maybe Father Alvarez...; she went up to her daughter and started removing the gown with a resignation nearing sadness; while unbuttoning the mother-of-pearl buttons she said aloud, good Lord, how lovely Manengo looked on his christening day; with the gown in her hands Doña Flora quickly left the room and closed the door once more; while she walked down the stairs she thought she could hear that same deep groan she had heard at other times, but she kept down and did not turn back; she hung the gown in the wardrobe and went to the kitchen to make some pea soup for Manengo's lunch and to concentrate on the cooking so that she would not have to think about anything; that night at the table Doña Flora refrained from making any remarks on her experiences of the day and they ate noodle soup and shredded meat with the customary antagonism and alienation; Manengo ate silently and the meal took place as if he had not been sitting there; Doña Flora spent Saturday night walking around the house in a state bordering on impatience; that night after the dishes she checked the clothes that everyone was going to wear to make sure everything was in order; on Sunday at six in the morning she was up and walked aimlessly around the house for such a long time that all of a sudden she realized she had to hurry to get breakfast ready or they would arrive late; the three of them had *café con leche* with bread and butter before getting dressed; when they were all ready Doña Flora went upstairs with the christening gown to dress Narcisa; she found her standing up, rigid, clutching the bars with an expression of anxiety on her face; Doña Flora dressed her hastily, without stopping to see how the gown fitted, without smoothing down the pleats on her body or checking the bows on the ribbons; she walked over to the chest of drawers, took the box that was on top, opened it near the crib and took out a pair of little white shoes and a pair of white socks; Narcisa anticipated her mother's gesture and without being asked she raised her right foot to get it shod, put it firmly on the mattress, then raised the other foot; Doña Flora lifted her out of the crib and placed her on the floor; Narcisa remained rigid, her

38

arms folded over her belly, waiting to see what was going to be done with her; Doña Flora took her hand and started walking towards the door; Narcisa let herself be led, she took a few steps along the hallway and walked down the stairs, trying her best to keep in step with her mother so that she would not be a hindrance; when they were downstairs Narcisa felt her mother letting go of her hand and she heard her say, Pascual, but Pascual, you're not going to listen to the radio now, are you? really, that's just like you; let's go, get up from that chair, or do you think I'm going to carry you to church? Don Pascual dared not answer his wife and as quickly as possible he went to the door, ready to go; Manengo followed him, for he did not dare contradict his mother either and he too was ready to go, standing behind Don Pascual; Doña Flora fetched the baby carriage, for although she did not feel like pushing it she thought that Narcisa would slow them down and that they would arrive late at church; as soon as Don Pascual and Manengo saw Doña Flora pushing the carriage they went out into the street and started walking; the four of them presented an immaculate picture: Don Pascual in his white linen suit, the one he wore to all the sacraments; Doña Flora also in a white linen dress; Manengo in a long-sleeved white shirt and black pants; and the bundle in the carriage in her batiste gown; there was a large crowd in the church, but many people had come for the mass that was to follow the christening; Narcisa knew exactly what the ceremony was about, and she decided that she would have to keep perfect

39

control over herself in order to endure certain unpleasant things, like getting wet and having to swallow salt; Pancha and Teresita were seated on the right-hand side of the church, on one of those benches that always smell musty; hey Teresita, do you remember when we came to the ceremony of the double sacrament? Teresita looked at her with a baffled expression, which double sacrament, Pancha? well, the wedding of those two over there, Flora was already so far gone that we were saying the child could have been baptized on that same day if the wedding lasted too long, because little Manengo over there was ready to come out; it makes me laugh because since that day the neighbors have called them the family of the double sacrament, and I tell you, Teresita, Flora pretends she's a ninny, but it seems she got so desperate after being engaged for seven years that she let Don Pascual do it, I used to have fun with Juanita across the street trying to guess where it was that Pascual had had Flora, and you know the best part? after he had her he refused to marry her and two of Flora's brothers set to work on him, because this serious gentleman you see over there was going to up and abandon both of them; Teresita made a face to intimate that one should not speak of such things in church, but she had waited a while before protesting, she had waited long enough to hear everything; Father Alvarez came in through the opening of the door on the right wearing an expression of dignity, almost of supremacy; Narcisa endured the whole ceremony without opening her mouth, as she had intended; during

40

the days following the christening Manengo abstained
from visiting his sister's room; more than ever he
concentrated on observing the various objects that fell
into his hands: a pencil, the chipped handle of an
enamel pot, a broken buckle, a piece of brown paper;
Narcisa remained standing, watching, hoping that the
door would open, hoping to be given a chance to
participate; but since the christening Mama had
prolonged her absences; she made an appearance when
she felt resigned enough to change her daughter's
diaper; Narcisa had started to notice a certain harshness
in her mother's voice when she came in and ordered her
curtly: lie down! Narcisa obeyed immediately, bending
her knees to reduce her height, letting her little hands
slide down the bars of the crib; Narcisa stopped
counting days, she stopped counting time; she was
distancing herself, leaving the christening day behind
her; gradually Flora complained less frequently: listen
Pascual, this is unbelievable, not a single compliment,
not even from Father Alvarez, not even from our
friends, you know what, Pascual, they didn't even
admire the christening gown! I didn't know where to
hide, Lord, I was so ashamed about the whole thing,
well, we'll have to resign ourselves, what can we do,
we'll have to bear this as long as God wants us to, after
all she's our daughter, you made her and I gave birth to
her and I don't think we should always keep her shut up,
after a while people are going to talk, just imagine,
Pascual, when our friends come and visit us they always
ask, and Manengo, how is he? but nobody thinks of

asking about Narcisa, it's just as if she didn't exist, but just wait, as soon as it occurs to them to criticize us they'll give us a reputation of being bad parents, indifferent, perverse or whatever; we should make up our minds to bring her down to the living room once in a while, especially at meal times; Don Pascual did not like the idea of having the bundle sitting in front of him, but he realized that his wife was right; he was particularly concerned about Armando's opinion, not only was he an old friend, he was also his boss at the Health Department; Doña Flora decided to let the day pass before beginning the struggle against a presence she would have to learn to accept; with some concern she studied the position Narcisa would occupy at the table; the system was already established, Don Pascual and Manengo sat facing each other and Doña Flora between them; the suitable place for Narcisa would be in front of her, between the two men; that way one could avoid Pascual being continually forced to look at her; next day at breakfast time Doña Flora thought it was too soon to begin the struggle she herself had initiated; maybe she would leave it till lunch time; she patiently waited until her husband had gone, for it was one of those days when she could not bear his presence; she walked to the door with him, in order to feel the relief of his departure; she returned to the living room, sat down in the rocking chair, she felt oppressed with an urge to let her thoughts run unhindered; fortunately Manengo was sitting on the floor, absorbed in the sight of a water worm swimming in frightened spasms in a little glass bottle filled with water; Manengo was turning the bottle around, slowly observing every one of the animal's movements; Doña Flora felt at peace, she reviewed her decision, she told herself that definitely, there was no other way; after a while she felt more at ease, almost liberated from an enormous weight; she got up to prepare pea soup for Manengo and she heard him shout NOT peas, NOT peas, but to Doña Flora's relief he quickly returned to the study of the worm's movements; at midday Doña Flora served a deep plate of peas for Manengo and one for herself; Manengo sat down at the table in his accustomed chair and cried, NOT peas, NOT peas! Doña Flora looked at him and striking the table with a banana she ordered: eat! Manengo uncrossed his arms, took the spoon on his right and began eating in silence; look, if you like, you can have a banana in your soup; and without waiting for Manengo's answer, she peeled the banana, cut it into small pieces and put the pieces in Manengo's plate, Manengo ate everything quickly and without protesting, he even seemed to enjoy it; after washing the dishes she looked into the living room again and saw Manengo sleeping on his back, his legs apart like a frog, squeezing the bottle with the water worm in his right hand; Doña Flora tried to take a nap but it was impossible, she was too restless to sleep; at three o'clock in the afternoon she turned on the radio without any real hope of hearing anything interesting; a few minutes later, to her surprise, a dramatic voice accompanied by organ music announced: and now, the first episode of

The Victim Unforgiven; Doña Flora was interested at once, there was a wealthy household with several servants, a butler, a gardener, a chauffeur, the master of the house Don Octavio Guzmán, his wife *Señora* Carmela del Real and Tatica the servant, *Señora* Carmela's confidante, with whom she shared a secret unknown to Don Octavio; Tatica, where do you think she could be? what color do you think her hair is? I wonder, what is her laughter like? sometimes I feel I'm going mad with that uncertainty that never leaves me; Tatica made a sign to call for silence, she repeated it with a warning: be careful *Señora* Carmela, I hear steps, oh God, I hope nobody heard you! the commercials broke off the scene that had become visual for Doña Flora and pulled her away from a drama in which she already felt so present, as if she had been one of the witnesses; during the commercials she could see Doña Carmela in her mind and she shouted at her as if she had been in the room: look at you pretending to be a lady, if you hide like this it must be because you've done something dirty, but don't you think you're going to fool me because I'm going to watch every one of your steps; when the narrator's voice returned, Doña Flora left off lecturing and became engrossed; during the second part of the program the action moved to an orphanage several miles away from the manor of the Guzmán del Real family; there was a solitary and melancholy seven-year-old orphan girl playing; a nun of the Caridad del Cobre came out on the patio and called her: Julia, come along my child, come in, it's time for prayer;

44

Julia, obedient and polite, replied with her characteristic refinement: I'm coming, Sister María, I'm coming just as you please; once again the music and then the commercials wrenched Doña Flora away from a story that she felt becoming hers; for a few minutes she remained so absorbed in what she had just heard that she could not return to the reality surrounding her; she continued to meditate deeply on the orphanage and on that little girl, she could not decide whether she should imagine her as a blond with blue eyes or with black hair and green eyes; but if that dear little girl was *Señora* Carmela's daughter, then one would have to forgive that woman and do everything possible so the child could go and live at the Guzmán del Real manor; good Lord, who wouldn't do everything in the world to help such a child, as for me, there's nothing I wouldn't do to help that child; after finishing this sentence she had to raise the corner of her apron to her eyes and dry the falling tears; after a while she got up from the rocking chair, feeling in her breast that wholesome fulfillment that comes from performing a good deed; she began preparing dinner with enthusiasm: chicken fricassee, white rice, ripe fried plantains; she even added an avocado salad she had been saving for the next day; after getting dinner started she proceeded to bathe Manengo, took her own bath and without giving it another thought she went up to fetch Narcisa to give her a bath too; when she opened the door she found her standing up and waiting, she spoke to her with a voice somewhat harsh: let's go Narcisa, I'm going to give you a bath; with some despair the little girl heard what her mother said, but she saw that she made no move to take her out of the crib; she waited prudently for a while, anxiously measuring the height of the bars; mentally she asked: help me, I can't get out, but her mother did not make the slightest move; then Narcisa knew there was nothing else to do, and she lifted her little arms to beg her mother to carry her; Doña Flora lifted her by the armpits, not noticing the sweaty closed fists in which was concentrated all the fear of being abandoned; Doña Flora set her upright on the floor and helped her go down the stairs; for the first time she took her to the bathroom that had been shared by the other occupants of the house before and since her birth; Doña Flora filled the bathtub and chose a small sponge that she was going to set aside for her exclusive use; Narcisa let herself be bathed in complete obedience, almost without a movement, except for a profound sigh which burst forth in gratitude and was accompanied by a heaving of the diaphragm; after the bath Doña Flora dressed her in a little shirt, a diaper and the beige kid leather slippers that Martinita had given her for the birthday they had not celebrated; Doña Flora went towards the rocking chair, followed by Narcisa; she placed her standing before her: look Narcisa, from now on you are going to eat and bathe like everyone else in this house; I don't know if you'll get used to it because the only thing you know are the milk feeding bottles you got regularly during the first few days after your birth; after that I was so busy, sometimes several months passed without my being able to look after you

46

properly, without being able to pay attention to your meals or to your other needs; from now on you are going to have to get used to eating, and you'll have to manage by yourself for your daily needs, but we'll start that tomorrow; for now, don't pester Papa when you see him, he's a man with a lot of worries and you mustn't bother him; Narcisa heard all this, her round eyes fixed on her mother, her right foot resting on her left ankle, making a wide angle with her leg; she had placed her left hand on her mother's knee and without having to agree or to speak she let her know that she accepted everything; obeying her mother, she sat on the sofa and amused herself by looking at her brother who was observing the water worm; Don Pascual walked across the room without looking in the direction of the sofa, without speaking to anyone; when he came to the bathroom he found everything ready: underpants, undershirt, bathrobe, clean towel, bath slippers; he went to the bedroom to get dressed and sat down at the table; at his right Doña Flora served the first plate, which she gave to her husband; Manengo refrained from protesting, for his father's serious face seemed to indicate that this time he was in no mood to make concessions to Manengo's demands; the second plate was for Manengo, the third one for her; Narcisa was waiting, her little hands clutching the utensils, a fork in her left hand, a large spoon in the other; everyone started to eat, Narcisa looked at every platter, she noticed that they were empty except for one in which there was a little rice left and another with two small pieces of ripe fried plantains; she thought that if she waited for the others to finish their plates they might clean up even those scant remains; she raised her utensils a little as if to call for attention; the others kept on eating, unaware of her gesture; then she decided to stretch out a little to reach the food; the effort was not enough, she still had a wide space to cover to reach the platter; then she decided to stand up on the chair, to lean over and, crossing the utensils like swords, she stretched, stretched as far as she could to catch all the grains of rice that could fit into her spoon; she transferred them to her plate; she proceeded also to get the two pieces of fried plantain; she felt equal to the others and she smiled at them without anybody smiling back at her; she cut the chunk of plantain into several small pieces and one by one she placed the pieces into the spoon with a few grains of rice; Narcisa enjoyed her first dinner with profound happiness; she thought that her mother was an excellent cook and that no other moment of her life or of others' lives could have been as beautiful as this one; she was conscious of forming an integral part of a perfect family, together with Mama, such a generous and dedicated housewife; with Papa, the supreme being on whom they relied for everything; with Manengo, so intelligent, so brilliant, a student of worms, jacks and other things, and there she was, the smallest and most beloved of all; after the meal, the table was cleared of mouths, forks, plates, tablecloth; everyone went about his business; Don Pascual went to the front room to read the paper and smoke a cigar;

Doña Flora went to the kitchen sink to wash the dishes, thinking, it's very pleasant to eat and all that, but those dirty dishes drove her crazy; well, one is never finished with this work in the kitchen; Manengo returned to the study of the water worm; Narcisa climbed onto the sofa to the same spot she had occupied before dinner; she got very close to the extreme right of the sofa, rested her right hand on its arm, stretched her legs over the seat; she felt important there, it seemed to her that her mother had told her to wait for her, that she would hurry to wash the dishes so that she could look after her as soon as possible; but Doña Flora finished the dishes, walked around the house several times, got Manengo's bed ready and helped him settle in it; she did not even come near the sofa; Narcisa continued wearing her smile of beatitude, repeating to herself that her mother did want to look after her and that she wished to care for her more than for anyone else, but what had happened was that she had gone to rest a little and had fallen asleep; she proceeded to get down off the sofa, managed to climb up the stairs, reached the open door of her room; she helped herself with boxes, climbed up over them until she could get over the rail of the crib and fell asleep, satisfied with her behavior at the table, happy with the welcome she had received into her family; that night she slept easily, free from those bonds which had oppressed her so often, tying her down at her ankles and at her wrists; she experienced how good it was to feel like this, free, suspended in mid-air, she rode through the night with a new feeling of safety; in spite of the permanent darkness of the room she was aware of dawn approaching, for she had learned to sense the break of day and the onset of the dew; she waited prudently for a call to breakfast, but Doña Flora did not appear; Narcisa was standing in the crib, firmly clasping the bars, her hands started to sweat, she was a little worried about the meal, as her mother had initiated her into the habit of eating and it would now be difficult for her to do without food, but her mother was probably busy and did not have time to come and tell her; instinctively she spread her big toe, forming tongs to grasp one of the bars of the crib, helping herself to climb up with the pressure of her hands; she did the same thing with her left foot; she scrambled up until she could sit astride the rail of the crib and from there she helped herself to come down on the other side; she had thought the feat would be more difficult than it really was and she was on the floor almost immediately, walking towards the door which she had left half open the day before; she applied herself to the job of getting down the stairs and she walked to the dining room with a light step, still a little faltering from lack of habit; the others were already there, absorbed in the task of devouring their breakfast; Narcisa climbed up on her chair and tied a napkin around her neck, a gesture she considered well-mannered; nobody looked at her, nobody returned the smile she beamed out as a first greeting of the day; Doña Flora looked over the tilted cup of coffee in her hand, got up, brought Narcisa a full cup `and placed a piece of bread next to it; Narcisa started dipping her bread in the milk as the others did, she raised the plump morsels to her mouth, they seemed delicious to her; after she had finished she drank the rest of the milk, pressed the cup against her nose and her mouth, waited a little while, as if hoping that more milk would come out; a harsh voice: are you finished? made her put the cup down and she met with a severe glance from Doña Flora, who was picking up the last plates; her father had already disappeared and Manengo had gone to sit in his small rocking chair where he rocked himself slowly, as if meditating on his plans for the day; Narcisa dried her hands on the napkin, untied it slowly from around her neck and placed it carefully on the table; she got down from the chair and went to sit on the end of the sofa she had occupied the night before; with her right hand she stroked the arm of the sofa as though expecting some kind of communication from it; from her seat she could see Manengo rocking himself in his little chair; she looked at him, he was absolutely motionless, then she saw him stand up, walk towards her, look at her fixedly, turn around, go away; Narcisa understood that he had come to fetch her; with her hands and arms she pushed herself to the edge of the seat, succeeded in getting down, letting herself slide to the floor, she followed him; they walked across the living room and across the dining room, on the way they heard their mother washing the dishes in the kitchen; silently they disappeared into one of the rooms, which Narcisa recognized as her brother's; Manengo signaled to her to keep standing in the center of the room, she obeyed, trying not to look around too much for fear of being taken for an intruder; Manengo walked towards the small chest where some of his clothes were kept; he leaned over to the level of the first drawer, which he pulled out jerkily, as far as his childish strength and the clumsy drawer that moved with difficulty would allow; when the opening was large enough Manengo put in his hand, started groping and from the opening he extracted a bottle filled with a liquid that Narcisa could not identify; Manengo sat down on the edge of his bed, examined the bottle attentively, turned it between his fingers; finally he opened it; he looked into the mouth of the bottle as if to see the splattering liquid while he moved the flask in his hand; suddenly he was motionless, he looked fixedly at his sister; he extended his arm to let her hold the opened bottle; Narcisa hardly moved, she concentrated, as if trying to guess her brother's intention; Manengo pressed his hand on Narcisa's and guided it, raised it to her mouth; a strange bitter liquid invaded her taste buds; she thought there was no way to escape her fate and she swallowed mouthful after mouthful without a single objection; Manengo observed the drops of sweat on his sister's brow with the same interest he had shown in the water worm; he saw the contents of the bottle disappear, he saw his sister turn a little pale, he walked around her in circles several times, he observed how his sister's right knee trembled and he saw her sink down and collapse on the floor after she had used her small hands as a buffer before falling; Manengo remained in the room a few more seconds to check what seemed to be a confirmation of the reaction he had expected; he walked to the door and vanished; Doña Flora and Manengo ate lunch without Narcisa, apparently not noticing her absence; at dinner time they saw her come, looking noticeably sluggish; she climbed up on her chair with difficulty; Doña Flora noted her yellowish paleness and haggard appearance and this frightened her a little, but she refrained from asking her if she was not feeling well; however, after serving the others their soup, she did serve a plate for Narcisa without her having to wait, to ask or to help herself; Narcisa ate the plate of soup slowly and felt gradually strengthened; nobody gave her anything else but she did not want any more; after everybody had finished she got down from the chair and went to her room, that night she dreamed of rows of monstrous harrowed faces, as thin as paper, which surrounded her crib and called her to account for her actions; Narcisa felt a certain uneasiness in her chest, a boundless urge to justify herself, so that all would know that she was not guilty of anything and that everything had an explanation; still asleep, she sat up in her crib, looking at the faces demanding justification; Narcisa was overcome by terror, she had no way of overpowering them and with a sudden gesture that surprised even herself she stretched out her right hand as if to try to communicate with them; the monsters went on with their scrutiny; Narcisa heard herself saying, lovely, you are all lovely, lovely faces; the monsters left the crib, moved away and vanished; when

Narcisa reached her fourth birthday her family actually decided to celebrate it; the transition had been slow and had required arduous and complex dedication; she had learned to speak clearly and with a powerful voice; she chose a way of articulating every word as she had learned long ago when she had lived in Doña Flora's womb or perhaps even before, when she had still been a shapeless mass in the universe; she had observed Manengo at table, his way of demanding the first plate with one gesture; she tried to imitate him so that she would not have to wait, so that she would not have to resign herself to the smallest portion, so that they would not always forget her at the time of serving; but her demands brought no results; then she experimented with the power of her voice, she tried it out, the sound reminded her of thunder; she thought she had an advantage over Manengo, the idea of being able to impose her authority with that roar of hers impressed even herself, but this too had no result; the first plate was always for Manengo, the next one for Papa, the next was for Mama, and she had to wait; her third birthday had simply passed amidst the indifference of the others; Narcisa waited during long hours, her eyes open and boring into the sleepless night, she imagined rings of shadowy figures dancing around her bed, expecting an answer; she tried to test the appropriate words, to articulate her sounds by using the most perfect vibrations; she spent endless hours of persistent and tenacious practice; on Saturday night at dinner time Narcisa came late to the table; she was anxious, her hands were sweating; she sat down and decided it was better not to increase her nervousness by thinking about what she was going to do; all of a sudden she stretched out her right arm, opened her hand and clenched it in a fist several times while she repeated: Mama lovely, Papa nice, Mama lovely, Papa nice; she hid her arm after pulling it back, observed her parents and saw their customary coldness gradually disappear; Narcisa took one more step: she smiled placidly to ingratiate herself with them; she extended her smile to Manengo, who turned his head aside to the left; Narcisa interpreted this gesture as a sign of approval; that night at bedtime Narcisa felt her hand being wrapped in her mother's large hand as they climbed the stairs, her mother was talking to herself about the daily chores in the kitchen and by the time they had reached the top of the stairs, about the need to buy a little bed for Narcisa and to move her to some corner of the house where she would be a part of the family, like everyone else; Narcisa refrained from making any remarks so that she would not have to make the effort of adapting her limited vocabulary to a torrent of ideas she could not yet express; during the following days Doña Flora applied herself to the job of convincing Don Pascual to buy the bed; she knew what it was to start buying furniture by instalments at a store, it was a business of never-ending bills, but maybe Chebo the carpenter would make them an adequate bed cheaply; Doña Flora began speaking at random: good Lord, we have to do something about that crib, it's getting too small for the girl and that room is so isolated from the rest of the house, well, it can't go on like this, it can't go on; Don Pascual's silence told her that even if her husband did not take on the idea with enthusiasm, at least he would not oppose it; and next day she went looking for Chebo, taking advantage of the fact that Pancha had offered to stay for a while and look after the *muchachos*, as she called the children, so she walked down Maceo Street; she crossed the triangle-shaped park, went on a few blocks towards Chebo's workshop; María Luisa received her in her slippers, dishevelled, unkempt in a cotton bathrobe that clung to her body a little, as though it was familiar with her unwashed skin; hello *Señora* Flora, come in, sit down, what brings you here? would you like a cup of coffee? I've just made some; Doña Flora declined the invitation, thinking the coffee had probably not been made under very sanitary conditions; no, thank you María Luisa, I've just had a cup at home, is Chebo here? María Luisa assented with a certain complacency at the thought that somebody who was almost important like *Señora* Flora had come to her house and was looking for her husband: Chebo! Chebo! come, somebody is looking for you; Chebo came into the little room in an undershirt, sweating, wiping his sweat with a handkerchief that had once been white; he held out his hand to Doña Flora who stretched hers out with resignation, restraining her revulsion at the sticky contact; hello *Señora*, what brings you here, what can I do for you? María Luisa, why don't you bring a little cup of coffee for *Señora* Flora; it's freshly made, you'll love it; Doña Flora apologized once more, no thank you, I've just had a cup, listen Chebo, I came because I need a little bed for my girl; something simple, not expensive, and if possible I'd like you to make me a mattress too, I've been told you can make them, and a solid frame that will last a long time, you know how children are, well, there's nothing I like better than things made on order, this way you get exactly what you want, how much would you charge me for it? Chebo felt so proud to have the opportunity of being of service to an almost important person that he gave her the best price he could calculate; listen *Señora*, since it's for you I'll charge you eighteen pesos for the whole thing; Doña Flora tightened her mouth a little as if she had expected a lower price still, but she did not dare protest, well, it's alright Chebo, I know materials are expensive, listen, I'll give you a peso's deposit, if it's alright with you I'll pay you monthly, one peso, half a peso, two pesos, well, whatever I can get; Chebo accepted gratefully and with satisfaction and promised to have the order ready within a couple of weeks; after making the deal he went back to the patio to finish planing down some boards for a chest of drawers he was making; María Luisa accompanied Doña Flora to the door and Doña Flora made her way back home, her face beaming because she felt she had fulfilled her mission, solved a problem; she came home and as a token of gratitude towards Pancha who had looked after the kids she told her every detail that could interest her: the size, the price of the bed, the mode of payment, the deadline for finishing the job, the

57

materials that were going to be used; Narcisa was still and quiet like an adult as she waited for her mother, her round eyes open, as if preparing to express surprise on hearing the news, but Doña Flora did not speak to her; after sharing the news with Pancha she walked past Narcisa without making the slightest remark, as though the bed had nothing to do with her; Narcisa felt that she had some difficulty breathing, but she soon told herself that there was no reason to feel bad, what more could she ask for? she was now part of the clan, she was an indispensable pillar of the family; the arrival of the little bed in Mingo's cart was an important event for Doña Flora: listen Chebo, tell Mingo the bed goes into that little room; a short while later the two men came in, each carrying one end of the mattress, walking rhythmically, trying not to miss a step; they went into a small room where Doña Flora kept an old sewing machine and a sewing basket; they propped the mattress against the wall, went out again and returned with pieces of the bed which they assembled, filling a part of the room with a wooden rectangle, with two legs protruding from the headboard, and another two legs from the foot of the bed, the springs and wire of the frame, the padded fabric of the mattress; the men went away before Doña Flora could think of offering them something: a cup of coffee, half a Materva each, a glass of water from the gallon jug on top of the ice-box, water that cooled as it passed through the pipes in the ice compartment and was almost ice cold when it came out of the faucet below; Doña Flora made the bed, she was excited almost to the point of tears by the new acquisition; the day passed without her making any connection between Narcisa and the bed, and when night came she saw her daughter's small figure slide down from her chair and walk to the sewing room, stumbling in her haste; she saw her look into the open door and stretch her arms before her, opening and closing her fists; she went up to the bed, she stroked the mattress with her right hand in an outburst of delight; Doña Flora brought her a little shirt, helped her change, helped her climb into bed; she saw her happy, covering herself up to her neck with the sheet, closing her eyes and preparing to go to sleep; Narcisa continued perfecting the praises she had learned to address to Manengo: *Ma'engo inte'igent, Ma'engo inte'igent*; Manengo would look at her with satisfaction as if agreeing with her; with every word of praise Narcisa became better accepted in the bosom of the family and when the time came for her fourth birthday, Doña Flora had to solve a problem: should she use the recipe with grated orange rinds for the cake or simply vanilla and a pink and white meringue? Narcisa was grateful for Mama's enthusiasm, especially as she knew that Mama was not feeling well; for the last few months her belly had been swelling, everything nauseated her, she vomited and she had dreadful fights with Papa: you must be happy to have given me this belly, Pascual; that night after Ash Wednesday I told you, don't, because it's Lent and it's forbidden to do anything till the forty days are over, but of course it's useless with you, when you're

59

determined to get on top you get there and nobody can talk you out of it and I thought this would happen, I told you so, you see if I don't get pregnant because of this shamelessness of yours, that's just what we needed, but you don't give anybody a rest, not even when it's ordered by the laws of the Church, is that really what you wanted? well, here we are, another bun in the oven and your salary still the same; Narcisa heard her father's voice speaking wearily, what do you want me to do? do you think with a woman in my house I'm going to look for whores at every hour of the night when I get the itch? no way my girl, if you feel like shutting your legs because of that Lent business, forget it, I'm not buying that; I'll put up with it from Holy Thursday to Easter Saturday at exactly ten o'clock in the morning, but that's enough and more than enough and as for your being pregnant, that's got nothing to do with me, you're the one who's got to watch out, just leave me out of this; these words affected Narcisa, for they differed from the perfect language her parents spoke to each other in her childlike imagination, where she re-invented them as beautiful, well-mannered, loving, intelligent; it hurt her to see them escaping from her and imposing a reality from which Narcisa had sworn to flee and to shut out from her private world; Mama tried to explain the origin of her swollen belly: I've got some beans in here and they've grown into giant beans and they're going to live here a few months, then a big bird called the stork will bring a baby in her beak, holding it by its diaper and that baby in the stork's beak will be another little brother

60

and when the baby cries for the first time, the giant beans will be so scared they'll get tiny again and so Mama's big tummy will go away; Narcisa looked at Mama, trying to conceal her amusement at that muddled tale about the reality of being born after being fed through the umbilical cord, after floating in the placenta, after slipping through the tunnel and choosing the Marsh of Zapata as the scene of her own first appearance; Narcisa felt a desire to penetrate the mystery of the foetus, and to achieve this she would use Mama's simple childlike language: please Mama, let me touch your tummy so I can see what the beans are doing; Doña Flora consented immediately, she was pleased to see that her daughter had believed her story so unconditionally: of course my child, come here, give me your hand, look here, touch here; Narcisa placed her right palm on her mother's belly; she felt the pulsations of the foetus, its heartbeats, the flow of the blood and she could hear with her hand, see with her fingers that inside, behind the swelling, there was a female; Narcisa gave her mother a laugh, trying to modulate it to an innocent tone while she withdrew her hand: thank you Mama, thank you lovely Mama; she left her mother, quickly went to look for her brother, she found him in his room, engrossed in a picture of Enriquito, the neighbor from across the street; Narcisa ventured to disturb him, for she thought her news would please her brother: Manengo, Manengo, it's a girl, the one who's coming is a girl; Manengo smiled with satisfaction and Narcisa understood the words which her brother did not

61

have to pronounce: I shall continue to be the king in this house, I shall continue to be the king; Narcisa left silently, she knew there was another bond of solidarity between her brother and herself; her fourth birthday came; the guests would start arriving at four in the afternoon; Narcisa asked Mama if she could take a bath and get dressed at three while she listened to the serial; Doña Flora refused to let her take a bath, for she had been late getting lunch ready and they had not eaten until 12:30 and so she would not be able to bathe until 3:30 in the afternoon after digestion was completed and as usual the guests were sure not to arrive before half past four or five o'clock; Doña Flora sat down near the radio and kept complaining the whole time about the awful program: well, you know, you can't expect programs like *The Victim Unforgiven* every day, that was a good one alright, I cried so much over that little Julia, good Lord, it looked like the child was never going to meet her Mama, but finally someone sent an anonymous letter to *Señora* Carmela del Real and if it hadn't been for that, God knows how long that child would have stayed in the orphanage, and one of the things that kept me from sleeping was that mystery of the anonymous letter, for which acquaintance of hers could have possibly thought of a connection between *Señora* Carmela who lives in a manor and the orphanage of the Hermanas de Caridad? I pretty much suspect who sent it, but as my luck goes, the day of the program when they were going to reveal the intrigue, for that's exactly what it is, an intrigue, well, that's the

62

day Pascual decides to come home early and at three he was already walking through that door and a cup of coffee and some cold water and get my bath ready and I want a snack and when I got back to the radio they had already gotten to Crusellas & Company and Hiel de Vaca soap, but what made that shameless rascal come at three? does he think I didn't know they weren't working at the Health Department that day because of the National Mourning? and that morning when he left early I played dumb so he'd go away and I'd be left in peace here, the same way I play dumb when he never comes home for lunch and he tells me he just eats a thing or two here and there, but come on, you liar, do you think I don't know you've got a hideout? I'm pretty sure it must be that Lidia the nurse, some tart she is, but if she fixes your lunch, look my friend, don't think I'm going to start crying, I've got plenty to do with the kids' lunch and mine; and that day he comes home with a face like butter wouldn't melt in his mouth and he says to me, don't you know, Flora? today it's National Mourning day and they let us off early; and it had to occur to him to get here just at the time of *The Victim* and I tell you, good Lord, the things one has to put up with and thank God at least I could listen to the last episode, the one when Julia, who's now fifteen, tells Sister María she wants to become a novice because she's got nowhere to go and her life is with the nuns from now on, well, without that anonymous letter *Señora* Carmela wouldn't have arrived in that monster of a car with a chauffeur in uniform to check up on everything and clear it up and when they finished out with the organ music and fell into each other's arms, she and her daughter, well, I cried my eyes out; but look what's on now, an office worker, a good-for-nothing clerk, this program is going to be a flop and I'm certainly not going to waste my time listening to it; and to confirm her philosophy of the moment Doña Flora went up to the radio and switched it off; in any case it was already 3:25 and the program was almost over, it was time for the music and the commercials; Narcisa was waiting obediently for her mother's consent to climb into the bathtub which she had already filled with cold water, for there was no hot water in the house; finally Doña Flora gave the order, get into the bath, it's getting late, and Narcisa quickly climbed into the water, soaped herself thoroughly with the washcloth, rinsed herself, dried herself, sprinkled herself with talcum powder and went to her room to put on a little yellow piqué dress that Martinita had given her for her birthday; Manengo demanded that Doña Flora get his bath ready, he shouted his order and Doña Flora remained silent while she ran water into the tub and brought Manengo a towel and the clothes he had to wear; at 5:30 everyone was ready, the guests started arriving; there were few of them this time, only the closest neighbors; the presents they brought for Narcisa went directly into Doña Flora's hands, she was too busy laughing and crying to remember that the presents were intended for Narcisa and that they should have been received and opened by her; Narcisa was content with coming close to her, she placed her little hand on Mama's left thigh and uttered intermittent and stifled exclamations of delight; they had already survived the emotion of a little rubber doll, of a can of Mennen talcum powder, of three small handkerchiefs, of a Kolonia, of two pairs of socks, of some delicate pink satin ribbons that could be worn with any dressy outfit; then there was a package so small that Doña Flora had a presentiment that it contained a valuable jewel: a little silver chain with a medal of the Miraculous Virgin or a gold chain with one of those little hearts that open up in which you can keep Mama's and Papa's picture; she had no time to imagine anything else, the box was wide open and everyone could see the present: two little white combs with Betty Boop on the part that held the teeth; Narcisa felt touched by magic, for her Betty Boop was a mysterious and unattainable figure; she made a gesture in the direction of the little box to bring nearer to her that black-edged outline and that bluish figure which stood out against the white plastic, but suddenly she felt Doña Flora moving away from her and her voice seemed unpleasant to Narcisa: and this, why did I get this? what do I want with this? with her thunderous voice Narcisa insisted eagerly, how beautiful, Mama, and the material is expensive, these combs are so expensive, let me see them Mama, you do like them, don't you? they cost a lot of money; Doña Flora made the simultaneous gestures of shrugging her shoulders, opening her hands, throwing her head aside and twisting her mouth to indicate that Narcisa had not convinced her; but Narcisa, with the

65

box still in her hand, went up to Charito, the
five-year-old neighbor: thank you Charito, these little
combs are so lovely, how lovely they are, did you see
how Mama liked them? did you see how she couldn't
speak because of the excitement she felt over these little
combs? Narcisa spoke so loud that Charito did not take
the trouble of replying, for her voice would not have
been heard and besides, she did not want to contradict
Narcisa on her birthday, she did not want to spoil the
beautiful moment Narcisa had invented for herself; I'm
glad you like them, Narcisa; the time had come to put
out the four candles on the vanilla cake decorated with
pink and white meringue; Narcisa walked over to the
corner where Manengo was sitting very still on his
chair, looking fixedly at Enriquito, measuring his power
over him from a distance; Narcisa wanted to take him
away from there to avoid the others noticing and seeing
what she was seeing, let's go Manengo, I'm going to
blow out the candles; Manengo got up, he made a
gesture with his hand to indicate that before going over
to the table he had something to attend to; Narcisa
followed him to the spot where Enriquito was sitting
and heard him say something about the photograph, he
seemed to be saying, I'm always looking at the picture;
Narcisa saw Enriquito cast a startled, terrified glance in
which there was also fascination; she walked over to the
cake, stood up on her chair, used her thunderous voice:
Manengo, come Manengo, I'm going to blow out the
candles; Narcisa put them out obediently, in one blow,
as Mama had ordered, and once they were blown out

she took out the small candles one by one, kissed them and started to hand them out: the first one is for my good Papa and the other first one is for my lovely Mama and now these two, this one here is for you, Manengo, and that one is for me; those on whom the candles had been bestowed felt flattered and they smiled while they spoke, thank you, my daughter, thank you my daughter, that's nice Narcisa, this one for me and that one for you; on the same plates in which the cake was served there were a few spoonfuls of the ice cream that Pancha had finally made with her ice cream churn, Lord, how she had fussed and talked about that ice cream, oh well, I'd better not start complaining now because it came just when I needed it most and at the christening we managed with the sour-sop punch anyway; with the cake and the ice cream there were paper cups filled with the Materva Armando had brought; Doña Flora kept the portions small so that they would have some left-overs for later; she did not bother to save any ice cream, for Pancha had not been very generous this time and besides, when the ice packed in salt starts melting the ice cream melts too and then that's it; when the time came to take the family picture, Doña Flora was a little cross at having to be photographed once more with that hideous belly of hers; Don Pascual was more serious than ever as he had spent the last hour silently watching every one of Manengo's steps, I think it's a fact, this boy is really a queer, let's see what I can do to straighten him out a bit; Manengo did not want to move from the chair where all alone he had consumed cake, ice cream and

67

Materva and from where he continued measuring his power over Enriquito; Narcisa took pains to achieve total harmony, this hand for Mama, that hand for Papa and you come along Manengo, come my brother, you have to be in the picture too; Manengo felt important when he heard that he had to be in the picture too and he stood up as if making a concession to the circumstances of the moment; through the lens their neighbor the photographer centered on a family unit that seemed inseparable and indestructible, he centered on Narcisa's image as he brought her into focus while he took shelter behind the camera; after a few seconds he decided that there was something radiating out of Narcisa, something almost beautiful; after Narcisa's birthday Don Pascual devoted himself to the task of watching his son, every one of his gestures, the sound of his voice, his way of walking; Manengo pretended not to notice his father's eyes, but in fact he felt them fixed on him; once in a while Manengo stopped and returned his glance, challenging him; on Wednesday after the birthday Don Pascual arrived with a package, went up to his son: come my boy, let's go to your room, I want to talk to you about something; in Manengo's room Don Pascual opened the package and handed Manengo a bat, a ball and a pair of baggy pitcher's pants, look what I've brought you, now you're six and it's time you played baseball; Manengo received the present in a conciliatory manner and even smiled at his father, as if thanking him; Don Pascual went on talking, encouraged by the success of his attempt: yes my son, you must play ball and let's see if this won't teach you to be a man, let's see if you don't become a real man once and for all; Don Pascual sensed an odd reaction in his son and he was unable to interpret it, but he realized that the moment of communication was over and he moved away, leaving behind a silence which soon spread over the room; when he came home on Thursday and Friday afternoon he asked his wife: did Manengo play baseball? the question annoyed Doña Flora each time she heard it: how should I know if he played baseball or not? do you think I've got nothing to do but spend the day watching Manengo to see if he wants to play? on Saturday Don Pascual retired to take his nap as he usually did whenever he happened to be at home at midday; he had slept an hour perhaps when against the wall of the room he heard blows that seemed to come from outside; he woke up with a feeling of triumph: these blows come from a ball hitting the wall, it's Manengo who wants me to see him play; Don Pascual put his pants on, fastened his belt, put on his slippers and went out in his undershirt to trail Manengo; he found him in the patio with his baseball pants on, covered with a short apron of Doña Flora's that dragged on the ground; Don Pascual came a little closer and he felt as though he could have killed his son: Manengo had made a small hole in the apron through which he had pulled out his penis and he was tugging at it in front of Don Pascual, shouting at him: look, you old hypocrite, is that how you want me to play baseball? Don Pascual unfastened his belt but Manengo took off the apron, started running and vanished through a gap between the boards of the fence; Don Pascual was left standing there, furious, but he was still able to think: a good thing he got away, because if I catch him I'll kill him, by God I'll kill him; he went into the house again, thinking that from now on he and his son had declared war for ever; at eight o'clock that night Doña Flora started feeling unwell, she was losing water; Narcisa heard Mama's alarm: Pascual, don't just stand here, don't you see what's happening? go, hurry up, but hurry up and get Esperanza, she knows this thing was about to burst, tell her what happened, but get moving, good Lord; Don Pascual put down the paper and reluctantly took his cigar out of his mouth, but he decided to take the cigar with him and smoke it on the street; Manengo kept aloof from everything that was happening in the house, he stayed in his room behind the locked door; Narcisa went to keep Mama company, Doña Flora was now lying on the bed on which she had placed a few towels; Doña Flora tried to tell Narcisa what was happening in an extravagant and childish manner, but Narcisa wished to spare her the effort, it's all right Mama, don't worry, get a rest, I'll keep you company with the contractions till Esperanza gets here; Doña Flora was a little surprised to hear her daughter speak with such maturity; Narcisa refrained from communicating her worries to her: I think this is going to be a dry delivery and it might be more painful than expected, I do hope Esperanza gets here soon; Narcisa remained at the bedside, sitting in the little rocking chair that had been Manengo's, holding one of Mama's hands,

70

feeling how Mama squeezed her hand once in a while as if to brace herself against the pain; Don Pascual came back with Esperanza who immediately went to Doña Flora's room and found her on the point of weeping: thank God, Esperanza, I thought you'd never get here and I don't know about this new one but I've suffered so much I think this is going to be terrible; if you weren't such a good midwife I'd be desperate by now; Esperanza calmed her down, she told her she was going to examine her and made a sign to call her attention to Narcisa's presence; Doña Flora hesitated for an instant and decided, look Esperanza, leave her here, she helps me with the pains and besides she can't see anything from where she's sitting; Doña Flora opened her legs to let Esperanza examine her; then the midwife gave her opinion: look Flora, this is still going to last a long time, so take it easy because we've got a long time to wait; the nightmare of crying, shouting, groaning and hand squeezing seemed interminable to Narcisa and then, around two o'clock in the morning, Esperanza's voice: push, push, push a little more, the head is about to come out; the next stage was relatively short; the pushing and crying became worse, then came the baby's cry, the cord was cut and what was left of it was tied at the navel; the baby was immersed in a basin filled with lukewarm water and the blood and all the fluids adhering to its body were washed off; Flora, I told you it was a girl, but what I didn't tell you is that she looks just like a little doll, look, what a pretty little thing; Esperanza brought Doña Flora the baby who was whining a little; Doña

Flora uttered her little laugh followed by tears: yes Esperanza you're right, what a pretty thing, a little doll, tomorrow if you can bring me an *azabache* for her, I'll pay you; Esperanza changed the towels, washed Doña Flora as well as she could, straightened out the sheets, took away the cord and the wash-basin and told Don Pascual he could come into the room; the baby was lying next to Doña Flora, she was dressed in a little shirt and a diaper: look Pascual, isn't she a doll, doesn't she deserve being spoiled and given everything? Don Pascual felt overcome by the obligation that the baby seemed to impose by her mere presence: they should give her everything, she deserved it; and without protesting that it was not a male, Don Pascual admitted: yes Flora, you're right, she's just like a doll, we'll have to please her in everything; Narcisa had gradually moved the rocking chair away and she was now sitting in the corner near the wardrobe against the wall; she felt her voice becoming hoarser and she was about to emit a howl, but she kept control over her vocal cords and succeeded in preventing the slightest sound from coming out; in a moment of profound meditation Narcisa felt the weight of the new task that had been assigned to her: she would have to please the baby; during the following days she observed her mother fretting about the feeding system, about the timetable she would follow for the baby; she saw her preparing feeding bottles punctually, at exact hours; she saw her organize the baby's christening so that it would take place two weeks after her birth and she saw her making her way to church despite the forty days of rest that are recommended after delivery, beaming amidst the compliments people were making about the baby; Father Alvarez blessed the family, he blessed the godmother Pancha and the godfather Quintín, Pancha's husband; Narcisa saw Papa and Mama enraptured with the ceremony, she saw how they were moved to tears when Padre Alvarez gave their daughter the solemn name of Florita-Ita; Manengo began attending the Marist Brothers' pre-primary school and Doña Flora thought it was about time for Narcisa, who was four years old, to leave the house; to be sure, Narcisa helped her with the baby, she gave her her bottle, she told her when the baby needed a change of diaper and she had even offered to change her herself, but I'm so scared she won't be able to manage with the safety pins and she'll accidentally prick the baby, good Lord, how awful it would be to leave a scar on that little body; Narcisa wants to help but sometimes I get tired of always hearing her: what do you want me to do, Mama? no, better if I stay alone with the baby, sometimes she sleeps so peacefully you don't even know she's here, if she cries it's just because she wants something but otherwise she never troubles anybody; Narcisa heard Mama explaining the situation: look Pascual, it's the best we can do, we'll send her to Domitila Prieto's little neighborhood school, well, she's the one who's really in charge, though Ernestina calls herself principal because the house where the school is located belongs to her, but you know very well that the one who manages everything is Domitila and I'm going to speak to her so she'll give us a reduction on the half peso a week because finding fifty *quilos* is not easy; Pascual was about to protest, he had twisted his thin lips, raised his upper lip to make a grimace of disgust, but he refrained from speaking when he heard his wife say, well, I really need time for the baby; if I don't look after her properly, who is going to? Doña Flora interpreted Don Pascual's silence as a sign of consent and the next day she put the baby in the buggy and went to the door after saying to Narcisa: look Narcisa, you'd better stay here, it's very hot outside and it could be bad for you; Narcisa sat down on the sofa and stroked the arm of the piece of furniture as she had done before; she knew it was time for her to enter into profound meditation, but she forced herself not to think of anything; Doña Flora walked happily with her six-month-old baby girl, stopping once in a while to acknowledge a spontaneous compliment for Florita-Ita or to beg for one each time she met a friend; the meeting with Domitila seemed a little dry to Doña Flora; she knew that she was a dedicated teacher and that she had the reputation of teaching well, but people were a little put off by that long face of Domitila's on which nobody had ever seen a smile; after the inevitable subject of the baby's beauty which Doña Flora had brought up herself, they went on to discuss the price of the lessons: look Domitila, tell Ernestina that Narcisa is still young, Lord, she isn't even the right age for school yet and how could she give any trouble? how much space will she take up here? we do care about our children, we want the best for them, but we can't pay more than three *reales* a week; the haggling continued until Domitila agreed to accept four *reales* a week, not a centavo less; Doña Flora left a little displeased, but she was soon happy again at the thought that she was sure to meet somebody on the way to whom she could show the baby; when she came home Doña Flora told Narcisa: Narcisa, tomorrow you'll start going to school; I won't be able to take you but it's very easy: look, when you go out you turn left, walk three blocks and turn right, then walk two more blocks and on the corner you'll see Domitila's house, I've already spoken to Domitila, she'll be your teacher; Narcisa opened wide her round eyes which she fixed on an undetermined point and said nothing; on the following day she took the piece of paper and the pencil that Mama had given her and left for school before the appointed time; on the first day of school Narcisa felt a little insecure, she was not sure they would accept her; on the way she thought of a solution: she would use her powerful voice to impose her presence, so that nobody, but nobody, could possibly ignore her and besides, she had to find a system, a way of pursuing her quest for the recognition of her virtues, a way of saturating other people, of invading their beings to such an extent that they could not escape from having to notice her, and this recognition would be visible like a scar; Narcisa was initiated into the knowledge of the alphabet; first she had to identify the letters, next she had to start reproducing them graphically; this apprenticeship seemed slow, very slow to Narcisa; with some despair she compared herself to the boys and girls who had started learning before her and who had an advantage over her; what distressed her most was the fact that Margarita could almost read; what hurt her most was to hear Domitila Prieto praising the girl: Margarita, you don't know how astounded I am to hear you read almost fluently, you're the quickest pupil I've ever had; Narcisa felt something thick in her throat choking her and she had to make a great effort to control herself when the teacher said to her: look Narcisa, you'll have to straighten out these letters, you can see they are leaning over and they are all twisted, look at the model carefully; Narcisa looked at her, widening her round eyes and Domitila gradually felt that the look of hatred she received from her pupil was penetrating her with something evil, like a malignant root that stretched through her body; Domitila refrained from contradicting Narcisa when she heard her say in her thundering voice: this A is beautiful, it's perfect, now I hold absolute control over the art of making letters and nobody can surpass me; when the thunder lasted for hours, with that same litany about the perfection of the letters, Domitila left the little classroom to have a rest from the incessant roar which tortured her; as soon as Domitila had left, Narcisa would go over to Margarita with a few pages from the notebook that had been bought for her, with a few pages filled with letters, such beautiful letters, there is nothing like these letters, the teacher Domitila may praise the others, but she knows, she KNOWS;

Margarita felt terrified by that imposition which encroached upon her being; she felt as though she had been in the presence of a mysterious force from which she wanted to escape; she could hardly endure that voice pounding space, coming nearer and nearer and smothering her; a few months after Narcisa's arrival Margarita and the teacher Domitila Prieto had vanished from the classroom; for the first time Ernestina made her presence known; she called Narcisa to a small anteroom: Narcisa, can you tell me if Margarita's and Domitila's absence has anything to do with you? Narcisa made her voice thunder-like, she swallowed large mouthfuls of air in order to perform the act of speaking, she gesticulated, she opened her eyes: oh no, *Señorita*, I couldn't, I couldn't, not for anything in the world, look, Margarita and I get along like two sisters and my teacher Domitila, I just love her, I've always said she was the best teacher; Ernestina was convinced by the emphasis, by the voice, by the grown-up manner and she answered almost tenderly: it's alright Narcisa, don't worry, it's alright, everything's alright; Narcisa left with a smile and sat down in the little classroom, wondering who the new teacher would be; she was filled with a certain satisfaction at the thought that she had impressed *Señorita* Ernestina, she was happy to hold power over that skinny figure under whose flaccid skin one could divine the harshness of the bones, over that long face, that grey hair in a bun on the back of the neck, those glasses mounted in a thin frame of platinum wire; Narcisa clutched her notebook as she walked, she

77

felt strengthened by the sentences pounding her brain: the technique of letters, I am the best, the perfection of my A's, my B's and all the other letters too, I am the only one who can do it and the shape of my letters is perfect; day after day when she came home Narcisa allowed herself to proclaim her new accomplishments, her new techniques in the shaping of letters and she earned the right to praise herself by praising the others: Mama, you are really a complete woman, there's nobody like you to keep house like this and you know, you are such a lucky woman to have a husband as perfect as Papa and a little doll like Florita-Ita and a genius like Manengo and I love you so much Mama, tell me if you are not proud of me, look at these letters; as she had so often in the past, Doña Flora felt like telling Narcisa in no uncertain terms that she should not bother her with the same old thing all the time, she should be quiet once and for all, she was tired of seeing those same twisted letters that had hardly changed since she had started school a few months before, but if Narcisa were silenced for ever, who would remind her that she was a happy woman, a complete woman with children worthy of admiration and with a perfect husband? of course, many, many times after being praised Doña Flora made Narcisa be quiet as soon as she started shouting about her technique of writing A's, but she had now learned to do so by means of some pretext: it's time for your bath, we're late for dinner, I have to change Florita-Ita's diaper; Narcisa would make an effort to close her lips over her gums and teeth and she left her mother, thinking, really, when Florita-Ita stands up in her crib her body looks so odd I can't see why they call her pretty dolly, with that bulging stomach of hers and those buttocks sticking out; why does Mama find her so pretty? because her face is heart-shaped like hers? why is Florita-Ita's crib in Mama and Papa's room? why is it not in the room upstairs? why is Mama always so anxious to put an *azabache* on her when after all she is the one who's always fishing for compliments for Florita-Ita and her friends are just being polite? and why is fighting and insulting each other a way of life for Papa and Mama? and why is Manengo always in danger of failing at school? is it because he is busy with those experiments of his? immediately Narcisa rejected the moment of profound meditation that had taken her by surprise; she went over to Manengo's room, which was immediately next to her own room and which was locked as usual; she ventured to knock, trying to gain her brother's attention by offering him praise: Manengo, my brother, open the door, I have to speak to you; Manengo, a little cross, opened the door and gave her no time to say anything: I've told you already not to disturb me when I'm busy, go and pester people somewhere else, can't you see I'm reading *Les Misérables*? Narcisa looked at the book that seemed enormous to her and lowered her voice to say, my brother, I am here to show you the technique I use to make my A's, you know that you are the brain in this family and you are the one who must decide; Manengo agreed, yes, it's true what you say about my being a brain, but your A is no good; Narcisa was grateful for the attention her brother had paid her before slamming the door, she thanked him for his solidarity with her work, she thanked him for his understanding; she went to sit down on the sofa to look at her letters while she waited for Papa to come home; when she heard his key in the lock she walked over to the door, she met him, not touching him: how was your day, Papa? I'm sure it was fine, wasn't it Papa? you're the best worker at the Health Department and all the women fall in love with you; while Narcisa said this in a whisper so Mama would not hear, she saw Papa smile with complacency: yes my daughter, Papa is quite a man, there's not a woman here who's not after me and since I am a real man...; after complimenting Papa, Narcisa took out her notebook, she insisted on her new techniques of letter-making; when she saw on her father's face that he was about to turn away from her she quickened the pace of her speech, barely taking time to breathe, she became agitated, she turned red, the veins of her neck swelled and she ended up vociferating: nobody knows these techniques as I do, nobody understands the process of making A's; Don Pascual was about to silence his daughter once and for all, but who would remind him that he was the best worker in the Health Department? who would remind him that there was no one like him with women, and one had to admit that on that score, he was a real man; he got rid of Narcisa with the same pretexts as usual: I have to take a bath, I must see Florita-Ita, where is Mama? where is Manengo? Narcisa went back to the sofa and repeated to herself that nobody, but nobody, was able to use the blank spaces on the paper as she did; from where she was sitting she could hear Papa: look Flora, I spoke with Armando today and I think he is right, Armandito's First Communion suit should fit Manengo and that's why Manengo ought to make his First Communion now, this way we won't have to spend money buying him a suit; Doña Flora put down the plates she was washing and raised the corner of her apron to her eyes in case she should start crying as she anticipated: good Lord, Pascual, I know all about it already, Martinita's just brought me everything, the pants, the shirt, the jacket, well, everything, and it's the boy's size, look, I've even got goose pimples from the excitement, you may not want to believe in miracles but to me it's like a dream; while he walked to the bathroom Don Pascual heard the little laugh followed by crying; several times Narcisa heard them discussing matters that she found unsuitable for the occasion: now, don't you take it into your head to order any of those holy images made of parchment, those fancy folded ones that look like books, the ones made of a single piece of cardboard are more than good enough; what are you saying? that I am ridiculous and stingy? and why do you bring up the subject of Armandito's holy images when you know that his father's salary is a lot bigger than mine? okay Flora, and why do you tell me I must behave on Saturday when Father Alvarez comes? if you have already told him to come over, well, let him come and he'll be well received because I'm no barbarian and I know how to treat people; that Saturday at ten o'clock in the morning a knock on the door announced Father Alvarez's arrival, the first to welcome him was Doña Flora who received him with exaggerated deference; when Don Pascual came into the room his wife had already begun the conversation: listen Father, besides having the pleasure of your company in drinking a cup of coffee, we wanted you to come and tell us everything about First Communion, as you know, our son is getting prepared and we would like you to guide us in what we have to do; Don Pascual was looking at his wife, thinking, that woman has got some nerve to make me waste a whole Saturday morning listening to that priest telling us things we already know; he had to control himself so as not to shout at his wife, you dimwit, isn't he getting prepared at school? what have we got to do with this? all we have to do is go there on the day and watch him make his First Communion; but instead of shouting what he was thinking he said: Flora, how about bringing us a cup of coffee? Father Alvarez had been thinking at the same time as Don Pascual: you dope, why did you call me? do you think I have time to waste on you? almost every Saturday I go and have breakfast or lunch with some wealthy family in town, that's something else and I know why I do it, but there is no excuse for this, really; one of the veins on Father Alvarez's neck was swelling from this silent shouting, but he controlled himself and said, thank you Doña Flora, what a good idea! Don Pascual, I'd just love a cup of coffee; Doña

Flora stood up, feeling very gratified at being connected with Catholicism like the important families in town, and they shouldn't think they've got exclusive rights over Father Alvarez, just look at him right here in our living room, he'll just love that cup of coffee I'm bringing him; when Don Pascual was alone with the priest he felt a need to confide in him: listen Father, I'm glad you came because there is something worrying me, I'll tell you frankly: you probably know my son is not like all the other boys, you know that I am a man, a real man, so as far as heredity is concerned, well, it's not my fault, it's impossible, but it is a fact, and sometimes I rack my brains trying to imagine what discipline and punishment one should use so he'll straighten out, so people won't be saying a son of mine is like this; can you imagine, Father? a son of mine like this? Don Pascual's last sentence was uttered while Father Alvarez was yawning slowly, hardly listening; almost without paying attention to what he was saying he answered, oh yes Don Pascual, the Brothers at school have already mentioned it, they say your son, though only seven years old, is different from the others, that in his body there is an adult already and it's just the same with your daughter Narcisa; you know, Don Pascual, the subject has been mentioned among several distinguished families where I go visiting, they say your daughter Narcisa at five years of age speaks like a grown-up, not only your son but your daughter too, but what does it matter if they are adults before their time? some might say, these are nature's whims; no, Don Pascual, you must say to yourself, that is God's wish and if you want something to help you, read over the Ten Commandments, read them again as I say and you'll see that there's nothing wrong with being an adult before one's time; look, to be honest with you, some people I know are surprised to hear them because children don't usually speak like this and as for your son, now I must tell you that the Brothers are not too happy with him: he pays no attention during Catechism and during prayers he is always absent-minded, in the clouds; and just imagine, they suspect he is reading *Les Misérables*, a book written by a Frenchman and I'll tell you something, when I left my village in Spain as a youth I knew who the French were, my village was a poor one but when it came to the French we knew who they were; and I tell you, I haven't read that book and I'm not going to risk committing a sin by reading it because I'm sure that title has been put on the Index at some time or other and I repeat, don't worry, people are saying that your son may be grown-up and all that, but instead of being first in his class, he is among the last, he's not interested in callisthenics or in calligraphy with the Palmer method or in Catechism, he is always making suspicious experiments and he reads books that are probably sinful, for if there's anything he did learn quickly that was certainly reading; Don Pascual, dumbfounded, was looking at Father Alvarez; Doña Flora came in with the cups just in time to hear: Don Pascual, are you surprised I know your children so well? don't be surprised, Don Pascual, that's our duty, that's our duty; although he had enjoyed it, Father Alvarez curtly said thank you for the coffee, told Doña Flora that the Brothers at the school would give her all the necessary guidance, stood up and hurried out; he might still get himself invited to lunch in some wealthy household where he would enjoy the delights of being attended to by servants, eating high class food, drinking a glass of sherry, of cider or perhaps that Viña 25 he liked so much; Don Pascual went outside to watch him leave and remained motionless where he stood, as if hoping that Father Alvarez would hear his thoughts: you numskull, how can you be so totally idiotic? what good does that cassock do you? Father Alvarez walked away and disappeared without looking back; Doña Flora called her husband in the haughty tone of a society lady: come in, Pascual, it doesn't look right, your standing outside gaping like that; people will say we're not used to visits from Father Alvarez; when he came in Don Pascual was a little put out on hearing the door of Manengo's room being closed, for he had thought that his son was in the patio with Narcisa, far away from the conversation and he decided to check this up; in the patio he found Narcisa sowing the seeds of yesterday's melon in a can filled with earth, she assured him, no Papa, Manengo hasn't been here all morning, but don't worry Papa, look what I am sowing for you: flowers Papa, flowers, lovely daisies to keep you company; on the following Saturday, the day of Manengo's first confession, his father took leave of him at the door and repeated: remember that you have to confess face to face like a man, that business of hiding behind a grate is for women; Manengo looked him straight in the eyes, Don Pascual ignored the cold silence and returned home quickly; in the confessional of the school chapel there was a long line of boys who were going to celebrate their First Communion the following day; a Brother split up the line and spoke to the boys in the half where Manengo stood: we are going to the church, this group will follow me and confess to Father Alvarez, many of you still have to go through and today we want to close early to go on a retreat; the Brother left the boys in the church; they had joined a line formed by men, boys, women and girls; the waiting seemed endless to Manengo, but he did not show impatience or absent-mindedness like the other children; he stood still, his hands folded before him, his straight black hair made him look like a rebellious Indian; brown eyes, a rigid and impenetrable attitude; the line had moved forward, it had become shorter ahead of him; a little girl whom Manengo thought too young to take part in the ritual confessed aloud that she had stepped on the tail of the cat her Papa had given her for her birthday and the day before yesterday she had eaten ice cream before lunch and she had not told her Mama for it was an act of disobedience and when she hadn't been able to eat up all her meal she had told her Mama she had a stomach ache and her Mama had given her milk of magnesia, wasn't I punished enough like that, Father? Manengo did not hear the priest's voice as he absolved the girl from the sin of stepping on the cat's tail and eating the ice cream but he saw her leave, her hands devoutly joined in prayer; Manengo came near the grate, forced an alteration in the tone of his voice, initiated the ritual of confession, heard the priest's answer and began, I confess, or rather, I should like to confess to someone who would understand me.that love between young men is beautiful and that is why Michelangelo carved David out of rough stone; Manengo almost forgot that Father Alvarez's ear was there glued to the grate, but the voice reminded him of the presence, of the cassock, of the greying hair: come now my son, don't talk gibberish, this is not the place to speak in riddles, get on with it, have you sinned or not? do you touch your private parts or don't you? the priest had asked for it, so Manengo decided to play the game: yes Father, every day, with Hiel de Vaca soap, made by Crusellas; the priest sounded impatient, and then, after the soap? I rinse myself, Father, with a lot of water, a lot of water; and then, after rinsing? a lot of towel, a lot of towel to dry myself, Father; Father Alvarez was angry and impatient for not having discovered any sin, he was about to dismiss Manengo when the latter interrupted: Father, I confess that I know the secrets of people in town; Manengo heard the priest moving on his chair to find a more comfortable position; tell me my son, what do you know? well, Father, I know I shouldn't talk about it, but this is about something I heard about Don Pascual and the Mondays of the goat of Moa, that's all Father, that's all I have to say; the priest urged him on impatiently, well my son, what are you saying about Don Pascual?

nothing in particular Father, it's just that eight years ago, when he was engaged to Doña Flora, she went on holiday to a farm in Moa; Don Pascual went to visit her every Monday night and after getting as close to her as he could, he got so frustrated after he had left her that he had to seek release with a goat at the farm, but on the last Monday of the holidays he heard at the farm that the goat had run away and so he persuaded Doña Flora to come out of the house that night after everybody was asleep and he waited for her at the same spot where he always met the goat and he got his release with Doña Flora and that calmed him down and he vanished on horseback into the dark of the night; Father Alvarez was petrified, unable to articulate a word, he tried to identify the voice hiding behind the grate; Manengo knew he was winning the game and said, well, Father, if you think my knowing about these things is so bad I won't tell you anything more, not another thing; Father Alvarez quickly answered, go on, my son, it's better you tell everything you know; Manengo waited a little before speaking, to heighten the suspense: well, this is something many people know, Don Pascual knows it too and he makes remarks about it, but I'm sorry Father, I'm awfully sorry to tell you about it because it concerns you; listen, I think it all started with the widow of Jacintico the saddler, she said that in a sermon of yours you had called yourself the Brother of the Plants and that's because under your cassock you've got two large mangoes, the widow said she saw those mangoes of yours herself the day you were eating green grapes with

Luneidita, the servant that Jacintico's widow had brought over from the country; well, the widow said that when you ate those green grapes with Luneidita she saw those mangoes of yours; through the grate Manengo could make out Father Alvarez wiping his forehead with a white handkerchief, he heard his faint voice: what do you mean my son, what green grapes are you talking about? well, I mean the grapes of the Ten Commandments, you know, when I asked Brother Jorge, what is fornicating? he told me, it's doing something you shouldn't, like eating green grapes for example, it's bad for you and that's what Jacintico's widow said, that the day you were fornicating with Luneidita she got home and saw the mangoes under your cassock; but that's not all, I can tell you some more; Father Alvarez felt that his fifty years were multiplying, he felt himself turning faint, he waited attentively but heard nothing more, he asked urgently, insistently, but received no answer; he decided to step out of the confessional and face the voice, but outside the box he met only the emptiness of the church; during the long confession of that boy with the weird voice lunchtime had come and the impatient parishioners had gone home to eat; Manengo's Communion took place without major events; Father Alvarez celebrated Mass in the school chapel; Don Pascual did not get excited, nor did he cry like his wife as soon as Manengo began marching down the aisle to the altar; the baby and Narcisa had stayed at home, Pancha was looking after them; when they had left the school Don Pascual remarked to his wife: didn't Father Alvarez look funny today? and without waiting for an answer, I thought he looked worn, upset, and what surprised me most is that he didn't even come to greet us and congratulate us about the Communion; Doña Flora was too excited to pay any attention to her husband, especially as she was now on her way to Aguilar's photography studio, for Don Pascual had agreed to having his son photographed by a professional photographer; during the following days at work Don Pascual heard that Father Alvarez was not feeling well, no one knew exactly what was the matter with him, he looked worried, hounded, at the same time he was harassing some people in town, talking nonsense that nobody could understand; this morning it had been Don Pascual's turn; around eleven o'clock in the morning Father Alvarez had come looking for him at the offices of the Health Department; the priest indicated a corner that looked private enough to have a talk: Don Pascual, don't think you are going to keep laughing at me because of those mangoes because in case you don't know, if you spread news about the mangoes under my cassock I know very well that you can mistake your wife for a goat of Moa and so we are even; the priest straightened his hat and set out to leave; Don Pascual sat motionless in his corner, unable to articulate a word; several clerks drew near, hey Pascual, what did the priest say to you? you know, everybody in town is saying he's not quite right in the head, it's not the first time he says that he might have mangoes under his cassock but that you mistake women for goats of

Moa; Don Pascual thought this was the time for maintaining his composure and his dignity and he shook off the crowd by walking to his desk; that night, not without some misgivings, Don Pascual remarked on the incident to his wife, but she attached no importance to it; she burst out laughing: good Lord, Pascual, just today Pancha was telling me about a joke that's going around town, men are saying maybe I don't have any mangoes under my cassock, but when it comes to being a man nobody can beat me; and they say when men get fresh, women know exactly how to tell them off: listen my friend, don't you make any mistake with me, I'm no goat of Moa; Don Pascual sank into a deep meditation, wondering about the origin of the gossip, about its transformation, its recasting and its metamorphosis into a local joke; Doña Flora went off laughing: that girl Pancha is a character, she's quite a character; Narcisa reached her seventh birthday, it was not celebrated this time, for the money was needed for clothes and care for Florita-Ita; when summer came Doña Flora started sighing and complaining as usual: Pascual, don't you think we could spend some time at the beach this year? I've heard the Viamontes are going to Varadero, well, I know this would be asking a lot, but can you imagine that fine white sand and walking there for hours and down there the water is never too deep? I know the sand is really like that, because Olguita's daughter brought back a shoe box full of sand and I even held it in my hands, it's so unbelievably fine and white, well, there's no use dreaming about it, but we could at least go to

Siboney near Santiago, even only for a week, even if we only stay in a cottage and the beach would do us all so much good! Don Pascual's face darkened and he said to his wife: you have a beach right here in Baracoa with fine black sand, what does the color matter and why don't you want to swim here? Doña Flora stifled her tears with the corner of her apron: because this is not what I call a holiday, Pascual, it's not a real holiday; during those three months Doña Flora suggested a few changes around the house, just imagine, Pascual, the girl is now three years old and she can't stay in our room any more, because when you get the urge nothing will stop you, even if you know the child is awake you get on top of me right there and then; the best thing would be to put the child in Narcisa's room and move Narcisa upstairs again, because just imagine, if we put two beds in the room downstairs who could put up with those stories of Narcisa's, nobody can stand them, good Lord, I feel like running away every time she goes on about the perfection of her letters and the perfection of her reading and of her language and the perfection of her behavior with us, well, enough is enough Pascual, just imagine her telling us that we live in perfect harmony, where did she get this, good Lord, when did you ever hear such a thing and I'm getting sick of it, every time the two of us have a little row which is as it should be and perfectly normal, afterwards we have to hear those exasperating speeches of Narcisa's that would drive anybody crazy and if she as much as suspects that she's often been a burden to us, then it's awful, you can be

92

sure you'll hear her for days on end, Mama, Papa, how nicely you get on, what a fine family, what harmony, how wonderfully you love me, but of course it's as it should be because my letters are so perfect and I am so good and nobody can look after you as I do, nobody can look after you as I do, nobody, Mama, nobody, Papa, because I am... I am... so beautiful; can you imagine, Pascual, that's exactly what she said last week and I tell you, it just makes me sick to hear her and if you tell her anything it just gets worse, she keeps repeating more of the same, can you imagine what's ahead of us for a lifetime? Pascual looked at his wife with a sharpness that she was able to interpret: why on earth did you give birth to that one? Doña Flora did not want to digress from the conversation about the alterations to the house and get lost in explanations about how little she had had to do with choosing the elements that had made up Narcisa, for the time being the main thing was to decide what alterations Don Pascual had tacitly approved; Doña Flora made up her mind to speak with Pancha, to bring her around to giving her goddaughter a little bed as a present; Pancha showed no enthusiasm at the idea of buying a bed for Florita-Ita, but she did speak with the Rosellós, who were about to move to Havana, to see if they would leave her the bed that had been Miguelito's, for Elba, Roselló's wife, had told her that the bed was getting too small for him; after a couple of weeks Florita-Ita was moved to Miguelito's white bed in the room next to Manengo's; Narcisa went back to the room upstairs where she religiously began shouting about her perfections, this was a ritual necessary to her life; Narcisa spent the first few days there recognizing her old room, impregnating herself with its smell, with every corner; she asked and was granted permission to have her bed at the same spot where her crib had been before and so she was able to situate herself again, to open her round eyes into the night and search in a point on the ceiling for the measure of her perfection; on the Sunday following the rearranging of the house Doña Flora organized an outing to Macaguanigua River amidst Don Pascual's protests, as he was forced to change his plan of going to the café with his friends and waiting for China, Manolo Quevedo's housemaid, with whom he was hoping to arrange a date, for it was said that China was generous with her body and he had already sent her a message through one of the sons of Güito the barber, saying that he would speak to her when she came by the café, but forget about it, when Flora gets something into her head there's no way she'll change her mind and even if I didn't go she would go anyway and what if she sees me on the street, what do I do? and I don't know how many times I've told her, Flora, if you like Macaguanigua so much just open the tap and throw as much water over your head as you like, this way you'll get your river right here at home; Doña Flora was in a wonderful mood; she had been to Mass at Our Lady of the Assumption, she had bought two pounds of mussels and some plantains to boil, she would cook lunch right there at the riverside and she had spoken to Palomo's two sons so that they would help her carry two small portable stoves, some coal, two cast iron pots and two folding chairs; Don Pascual had stayed at home to look after the children so that he would not have to go to Mass; when she came home Doña Flora met Florita-Ita who was happy, ready and willing, as if the outing had been organized especially for her; Manengo was in Narcisa's room, giving her instructions: we don't need a clock because I can estimate time, I don't want her to drown, I only want to know how long it takes her to become unconscious; Doña Flora and Don Pascual had their folding chairs placed under a tree; they saw Palomo's sons move off, barefoot, dirty and ragged, the eldest clutching in his hand the *medio* they had been given to share between them; Don Pascual shouted after them: at five o'clock sharp! come back at five! and sat down, pressing Doña Flora to start cooking; Manengo and Narcisa took Florita-Ita to the riverbank, each holding one of her hands; Florita-Ita let herself be led into the water with the delight of a spoilt child, she felt her brother and sister holding her firmly; Florita-Ita believed herself safe and protected until her brother's hand fell heavily on her head and pushed her to the bottom; Narcisa was also holding her down so that Florita-Ita's head would not come up for air; within a fragment of time, which seemed long to Narcisa, Florita-Ita's body stopped struggling and both felt it becoming completely still; while hauling his younger sister by the hair to pull her out of the water, Manengo· said to Narcisa: just as I thought, it took her exactly the time I had figured to

95

become unconscious; you revive her, I'll distract Papa's and Mama's attention; Narcisa was left alone with the child who was lying face down on the ground; she thought of some outlandish exercises to stimulate her breathing and make her spit up the water she had swallowed; Narcisa told herself that it was she who had saved the lives of so many people drowning in the Nile, she had brought her knowledge down with her across centuries and through each of her reincarnations: she placed her legs at each side of Florita-Ita's waist, began with something which at first sight appeared to be an insignificant massage and began a litany: you cannot drown today, Florita-Ita, you cannot drown today; the child began coughing, the water spurted out of her mouth, she started moving slowly, as though waking from a deep sleep; Manengo was talking to Papa and Mama about the founding of Baracoa in 1512 by the governor Diego de Velázquez, he told them about the Indian origin of the name; while walking between the tree and the camp stoves where the mussels and the plantains were cooking, Manengo repeated that it had been the first Spanish city, later it had become the national capital and in 1838 it had been given the name of The Very Loyal and Famous City of Baracoa; Manengo was about to speak of the first church founded in 1511 in La Punta, he was going to speak about the wooden cross supposedly brought over by Columbus which had later been called the Cross of the Vine because it had been lost and someone had found it again near a vine, but he saw Narcisa coming, holding the child's hand and he stopped talking, his parents weren't paying attention and he did not wish to share his stories with them in any case; Doña Flora left the pot of mussels and walked up to Florita-Ita; for heaven's sake my daughter, good Lord, what happened? why on earth do you look so ill? Narcisa quickly explained, nothing happened Mama, she is so little and the sun and the water tire her in no time; Doña Flora sat down, took her daughter in her arms, the child put her arms around her and fell asleep; at five o'clock Palomo's sons came to take the things away and to get the other *medio* they had been promised; Don Pascual had to carry Florita-Ita: let's see, my child, what's the matter? just as I thought, exposing this poor little child to this hot sun, who would think of doing a thing like that? that night Narcisa found it difficult to go to sleep; images rushed in, jostling one another to make their way into her mind, not waiting for their turn in the order of sequence and all crowded in at once into her mind, trying to take possession of it and turn it into a multiple stage; everybody seemed to be asleep, they were all asleep, but there they were, besieging her without exercising their conscious will; Papa's thoughts, filled with anger and resentment about the lost date with China pounded her brain; Mama's thoughts besieged her too, they were less angry and less resentful, for even though Macaguanigua isn't Varadero Beach, still, a summer trip is a summer trip; then the baby's thoughts came and hammered their fatigue into Narcisa, their foggy confusion, their sudden resolution to remain buried in sleep; Manengo's thoughts hammered on her brain, they were stubborn, limited, rebellious thoughts, how can those two understand anything if they can't even get into their heads the simple notions of history or dates or the importance of understanding the phenomena surrounding us; in a moment of profound meditation Narcisa realized that she would not be able to survive her metamorphosis for very long, her transformation into a multiple stage where all the others lived inside her; slowly she walked to the door of her room, walked down the stairs and proceeded to return the thoughts to their owners, in the order in which they had appeared; she stopped by the side of the bed where Papa was sleeping and in a very low voice she began a litany: keep the children of your mind to yourself, do not let them devour the fragile land of my being; she went to the side of the bed where Mama was sleeping: keep the children of your mind to yourself, do not let them devour the fragile land of my being; she left her parents sleeping fitfully; she went over to the baby, trying to feel tenderness for her, but all she felt was coldness: keep the children of your mind to yourself, do not let them devour the fragile land of my being; she stopped to look at her sister who was sleeping on her stomach, she saw her start up and raise her little body slightly, helping herself with her hands, she saw her open her eyes and suck her lower lip a few times as if she were about to cry, she saw her close her eyes, lie down again and go back to sleep; Narcisa walked away and looked for Manengo; she stopped in front of him and was silent for a long time; without moving her lips she let him know: brother, take back the thread of your inner voice so that it will not get lost in the fragile land of my being, in you the destinies of Antiquity are being fulfilled; Greece, Mesopotamia, Egypt have been extended into your fingers; leave your body and follow me, let us penetrate the secret of our land; Narcisa became a voice, she transformed her brother into sound, they left the precincts of the house, they became inhabitants of the night: when I underwent my metamorphosis in the Bay of Maisí I wanted to occupy space in another shape: I wanted to go up to the lighthouse and from there soar over the black reefs, over the sand terraces, over the caves where you would have probed the mysteries of the Indians, follow me, today we shall complete our journey; followed by the wail of the wind, Narcisa traveled across space to Maisí, they alighted at the appointed places, the voice guided them once more: come with me, our land is calling us, this land which knows the secret of our fragile being; Narcisa alighted at the entrance to the bay, at the Black Stone of Burén; the wail of the wind became a rumbling of waves; Narcisa told him, it is time for us to feel like this stone, we are the infinite freedom of its atoms, we are its stubborn hardness; let the miles that separate us vanish and from here let us be the flat land of the Yunque; let us be the sweet dampness of its hillsides, let us break the law of symbiosis, let us be part of its earth while we abide here; the voice was silent for a while, as if to permit the process of synthesis to take place and once more it was heard at the Burén: come with me, my brother, let us live in the lighthouse of Barlovento Point, there we shall grasp the mystery of the ellipse; we shall go to the castle which has changed its names in several strokes of time: Baracoa Castle, Seboruco Castle, Sanguily Castle; we shall be the mortar in its walls, from its height we shall be a vision embracing the roofs that cover the houses of our city; the rumbling of the sea became roaring of the air and it followed the voice; they came to the end of the journey; voice and roar cease for an instant, come my brother, today you will understand the mystery of the *tibaracón*; I shall be your elongated delta on the coast and you will be the current parallel to the sea and you, River Macaguanigua, will have to find your way to the sea; Narcisa was a voice, the arms of a voice, a sand-voice spreading out into a delta, she saw her brother running, she heard the voice of his current, she felt the movement of his course, further, you must go further still, you must flow into the sea, you must cut through the delta, cut through the delta and flow into the sea; the vertiginous movement stopped with a sudden blow; Narcisa felt the abrupt weight of her materialization, she found herself on the floor in Manengo's room, she stood up, she walked towards her room; she left her brother asleep and now at one with his astral body; Narcisa climbed mechanically up the stairs; she let herself fall onto the bed, she slept peacefully; during the next few days Narcisa remained thoughtful and silent, she was careful that no one should break into that inner state that was sealed within her; until the fourth day after this experience Manengo had stayed away from her, hardly speaking to her; on the sixth day Narcisa felt that the retreat had run its cycle, she sought an opportune and solitary moment to speak to her brother: today is the sixth day since our journey to the mouths of the earth, I wanted to guide you, I wanted you to become movement, sound, air, light; Narcisa had spread out her arms, the gaze from her round eyes had become uncertain, prophetic, she had not noticed her brother's resentment, his near hatred until she heard: what you call our journey was a dream, an illusion in which I had no voice, what right have you to think that I can appear voiceless on the earth? Narcisa moved back a little, kept her arms outspread and spoke: you were the voice of the air, you were the voice of the sea, you were the voice of our river; Manengo tightened his right hand in a fist at the height of his thigh, he shouted: who are you to presume you can be my guide; who are you to ascribe destinies to me on this earth, don't you dare attempt to grow to my level, don't you dare try to break the limitations of your miserable human condition; Narcisa watched her brother go away, she remained motionless until nightfall; she heard her father coming home, she heard Florita-Ita's noisy excitement because Papa had brought coconut *cucuruchos*; that night she ate silently and withdrew to her room; during the course of the summer it was arranged that Narcisa would attend the Colegio Cervantes in September, because just imagine, Pascual, she has reached school age and what will people say if we send her to a public grade school? if you get a higher

101

salary, and it looks like you're going to get it, if not why would you have gotten a visit from the inspector? if you do get that higher salary we won't have any problems paying for her schooling; with some annoyance Don Pascual remembered Armando's visit the previous Saturday: Pascual, I want to talk to you about your situation at the office, this time it's serious, there's talk of transferring you, even dismissing you; Don Pascual quickly kept his wife back before she could enter the living room: Armando and I have to talk, don't come into the living room, this is men's talk; Doña Flora was happy not to have to wait on Armando, for at this time, at three o'clock, there was a variety program and some poems by José Angel Buesa, they recite them so nicely, that one about "you will come into my life without even noticing that you came," I don't want to miss it; Armando found it difficult to begin the conversation: look Pascual, I came to see you because of the complaints that have reached the inspector who came from Havana for a few days; several secretaries have complained that you touch them when you walk near them, I know this is not important, but the complaints of some of the ones who are angry with you... they talk about transferring you, they talk about dismissing you, they also complain that the jokes you tell are a bit too coarse, I'm sorry about all this but what can I do except warn you? Pascual's face remained wooden, impenetrable; he walked to the door with his friend; on taking leave he shook his hand vigorously; Don Pascual was thinking, so that's what the inspector was after with all his questions, where do you live? well, on Maceo Street, it's between Maraví and Tenth of October Streets, I don't know if you know the town, Inspector, it's near the Church of the Assumption, the one in Independence Park, that triangle-shaped park, we live three or four blocks from there, near the Post Office, near the Encanto Cinema, we've got everything there, it's right at the center of town; yes, I have children, the youngest is nearly four, the second is almost eight, the eldest is ten, is that all, Inspector? well, it's a pleasure; Don Pascual felt cold sweat running down his back, so that's what the inspector wanted to see me for, well, fortunately Armando seems to have settled the matter; on Santiago and Santa Ana's days, on the 25th and the 26th, there would be dances at all three clubs of the city; Doña Flora walked incessantly around the house; it was the month of July, it was hot, "impossible weather," as Don Pascual said, and the heat made her walk about restlessly and besides, who could feel calm thinking that after so much hassle just a few months ago I finally got Pascual to become a member of the Liceo and now we have a chance to go to a dance already, good Lord, how bad I felt when Martinita told me that on the thirty-first she was going to celebrate New Year at the Liceo dance and she was going to another one on the sixth of January and Flora, I'm just so busy getting the children ready to go to the Epiphany dance, and I couldn't even tell her, well Martinita, it's just the same with me, but everything comes out right if you're patient, I must speak with Lourdes, Miguelón's daughter, so she'll spend the night here and look after the kids, I know she'll be happy to if I give her a meal and a few pennies; now you can be sure Martinita's going to buy a dress at La Francia on that trip to Santiago she's thinking of taking and afterwards she'll just come and show it to me as though it were nothing at all; well, with what Pascual brings home there's hardly enough left to buy a length of crepe at the Pole's remnant shop and so I have to tell the seamstress Candita that I'll help her with the finishing so that she will charge me less for making the dress, good Lord, of course I can manage a hem and finish off the seams and pretty well too; but if I say a word about it to Pascual he'll say the last piqué dress I got her to embroider for Florita-Ita was one too many, but good Lord, how lovely she looks in that dress, how lovely; Doña Flora raised her apron to her eyes in case she felt like crying over the piqué dress; but she soon got hold of herself again, thinking determinedly that at the dance on the 25th she would wear a new navy blue crepe dress with white floral designs and she was already imagining what it would look like, I can see it as if I had it right here before me; Don Pascual offered less resistance than she had expected and he approved the purchase of the dress, for after all, a woman represented by him at the Liceo should look nice; they had decided to go to the dance celebrating Santiago's day; Doña Flora wore her blue crepe dress with white floral designs and a layer of powder that made her face look white, a little like the rice-powdered mask of a Japanese geisha; Don Pascual had on his white linen suit; without really wanting to they stayed together, one clinging to the other, when it was time to fetch punch, when they got cider, when they bought a ham sandwich, when they went to the bathroom where they parted below the signs "ladies" and "gentlemen," vanished through the adjoining doors and met again when they came out; Don Pascual secretly regretted not being with his friends at the café, where he would certainly have been the center of attention with those daring jokes of his that he kept in reserve for every opportunity, but this, this here is really unbearable; Doña Flora did not permit herself the slightest remark, not even a silent one, for that's what you have to put up with if you want to have class, that's how it is, you must belong to society; Doña Flora did not let herself admit that this business of trying to belong to society was demanding a great effort from her, it made her feel tense and she used to feel better, but a lot better and in fact she had felt really happy on all those Sunday afternoons when Pascual went off to the café and she would grab the three children and even if it was pouring with rain they would go to the Encanto Cinema for the matinée and she got the money for the movies some way or other and if she hadn't managed that she would have missed *The Song of Dolores* with Imperio Argentina, a great movie I'm telling you, and now that I've seen the preview for *Quinto Patio* with Emilio Tuero I'm saving money to go next week and if it's in English, well never mind, I just read the captions, how I cried at *Love Letters* with Jennifer Jones and Joseph Cotten; she was

105

interrupted in her meditation on her favorite movies by Martinita's voice: hello Flora, how are you Pascual, I'm so happy to see you; but she did not stay to talk to them; Doña Flora was looking at her gray gauze dress: that Martinita really looks good, of course when you wear clothes from La Francia it's easy to look good, but I must admit she's got a nice figure, she really does, good Lord, look at that slim waist, of course if you're thin like that everything looks good on you, I'm sure she's now going over to talk to the mayor, Ricardo Pérez Morgado and his family and that's how it should be, one should talk with people who can be useful to you, but since 1940 when Narcisa was born, I'm behind that husband of mine, Pascual, do try to be a bit sociable with Leovigildo Prada Lores, and after Leovigildo had gone past us I told him again, try to be sociable with Manuel H. Galano Coutín, because, good Lord, if you don't make friends with mayors, where will you get support? but there he stands, not speaking a word to anybody and it's always the same with him, all he ever wants is to go to the café with his friends and he thinks that just solves every problem; suddenly Doña Flora realized that her glass of sparkling cider was getting empty and she was about to ask Pascual to go and fetch her another one, if only to have something to do, so that at least the others would see her raise her glass to her lips and drink, but at that moment the couple representing "Perla de Oriente," the club for mulattoes, and the couple representing "Progreso," the club for blacks, came into the room, they were going to dance one round according to the

106

custom and afterwards they would go back to their respective clubs; Doña Flora watched the two women in their tight satin dresses undulating to the sound of a *danzón* and she thought, those blacks really have talent for dancing, you've got to hand it to them, but they overdo it with the glitter, I'm sure they'd be wearing those satin dresses even if it was eleven o'clock in the morning; when the dance was over the public applauded the orchestra and the two couples who came off the dance floor shortly afterwards and disappeared; after a few dances the orchestra took a few minutes' break; Doña Flora went on raising her empty glass to her lips, just to do something; when the orchestra started playing again she spoke to her husband: come on, Pascual, we should dance, even if only once, otherwise what are all these people going to say, that we are not used to society? Don Pascual got up reluctantly, stretched out his left arm, placed his small frame at a distance he judged prudent, tried to follow the rhythm marked by the flute, heard his wife's voice coming down from above: good Lord, Pascual, what a weakling you are, I don't even have the feeling you're leading me, but what on earth are you doing? can't you see how the others dance? look at Armando and Martinita, look how well they follow the steps, but you, you just drag your feet from one side to the other, you think that's enough and one doesn't even know which side you're going; I understand your not liking to dance *boleros*, because you are in your forties already and I'm not far behind, imagine what we'd look like dancing cheek to cheek, well, even the young ones are really beyond the limits of decency nowadays, I've seen some squeezing here, I tell you, what's that? I make you mix up the steps with my chatter? Well, I'll tell you what, let's sit down right away, you've been stepping on my feet so much, it's unbearable; the *danzón* stopped, Doña Flora walked up to the chairs with her husband, fanning herself vigorously, although at that moment with the electric fans whirling on the ceiling, the heat had subsided; from September on Narcisa walked to school regularly, her books tied together by a leather strap fastened with a buckle, the other end of the strap around her hand; Narcisa sometimes wondered why the four friends who had not spoken to her for the last few months had not come to make peace with her after she had announced at Domitila Prieto's school that she would not be back in September; she remembered the circle they had formed around her one April morning in the empty school yard; the four of them had made a ring, extending their arms and holding one anothers' hands, and Narcisa had stood in the middle; one of the voices began the litany, it chanted a fragment alone, then another voice came in, added another fragment and repeated the preceding one; another voice was added to the third and in the fourth part all four voices were chanting together: we refuse/ we refuse to tolerate/ we refuse to tolerate your voracious need/ we refuse to tolerate your voracious need for recognition; with an abrupt movement the hands were released, the circle was broken, Narcisa saw them move away, she felt time and distance separating her from them; her friends' determined attitude had paralysed her, had arrested the flow of words that crowded into her astonished round eyes; during her moments of profound meditation Narcisa knew that the abandonment she had suffered in the school yard was a symbolic abandonment which had tried to materialize, to encircle her and mark her with a seal, and a question arose from her meditation: why do they forsake me? why do all forsake me? is this my destiny being fulfilled? an inner voice dictated the answer: no, they forsake me because they do not understand, they do not know who I am, they do not know how I feel, they do not understand my world; I am an incomparable, unique daughter and sister, my world is that of harmony and love, I represent a state of perfection in the universe and I live in holiness; Narcisa felt an invigorating force running through her veins and before she had seen the last of her friends vanish into the classroom she felt revived, in control of reality, of the only reality she recognized; on that day she insistently participated in all the classes of Berta Sugragnes, the teacher who had replaced Domitila Prieto; at her new school Narcisa imposed her presence unnecessarily by shouting as she did, for we know you shall attract proselytes, followers, friends drawn by your enthusiasm in discovering the essence of things, seeking your multifarious and complex ability to interpret your predicament, to analyze the components of that predicament with accuracy and to assign it a suitable position within a scale of values; we know you can solve mysteries, cut a passage through closed doors, bring to our levels of perception the rich experiences that ordinary beings do not notice; take the miracle within the reach of your hand, a single gesture will be enough, we shall follow you, we should follow you, the students around you will follow you, we ourselves shall follow you, we shall become a page and walk by your side letter by letter, at your pace; Narcisa's desk stood in the middle row of the classroom; she was pleased with her teacher *Señorita* Estela Guzmán, a young woman with an olive skin and soft almond-shaped eyes, of course I like her, for she is within the reach of my voice and if I roar in the classroom she always pays attention to me, she gives me an answer, she makes some gesture of communication, at this very moment she is writing titles for our essays on the blackboard, gardens and plants of our city, typical dishes of Baracoa; the *tibaracones*; the course of the Toa River; the nickel mines; the legend of the Cross of the Vine; my favorite mayor; my family; yes, *Señorita* Estela, that's the subject for me, *Señorita* Estela, may I choose "My Family"? of course Narcisa, you may choose your family; and she continued writing on the board: my birthday; portrait of a friend; commentary on "The Two Princes" by José Martí; on her way home Narcisa thought about the ideas she would use in that essay on her family; that night she went to her room early, she sat down on the bed, her back leaning against the headboard, squatting, with a pad of lined paper on her knees; at the top of the page she wrote: "The Family," crossed out part of the title, wrote again and read aloud: "My Family" and began: where do the souls of our dear ones come from? what is the origin of the nucleus of this cell formed by the atoms of Papa, Mama, my brother Manengo, my sister Florita-Ita and myself? we must go back to far away times, to epochs when the sextant was the fundamental instrument; we must go even further back, to those times when papyrus navigated over the oceans in the shape of floating cradles that transported the discoverers of continents now lying at the bottom of the sea; one should not study history, but simply look at it in a succession of flashbacks; the soul of my brother Manengo was born and grew out of Assyrian kings, my brother Manengo is branded by the seal of the gods, my brother has come to reign here under the title of The Crowned One; Florita-Ita's soul grew out of the mountains of Toa, out of the spring of our long swift river where canoes gather and bring the harvest from the high regions of the interior, she is a young soul, transparent and deep, alien to frivolity; my Papa's soul was born of tobacco leaves; he floated through the air from the region of Vuelta Abajo, so that he would become an example for our city, a protector for our family, a mainspring of energy for our spirit; Mama's soul rose from the bottom of those ancient cauldrons where the first generations of creoles boiled plantain leaves to wrap *bacanes*, she came to our family to give us liberty of thought, to give free rein to our evolution; my soul was born of the particles of sand that flew from the eroded face of the Sphynx; we are five pillars, in

111

cabalistic number, we occupy a harmonious space filled by our sanctity; the light of day caught Narcisa asleep, still squatting on her bed; her right hand was open, in it lay a yellow-painted black lead pencil; Narcisa spent the following days copying her essay until it was free of all blemishes, at home she refrained from making any allusion to it, saving the excitement and the surprise for later, when the teacher would compliment her and she would bring it all as a present to her family, the essay and the laudatory comment; at home and at school she waited silently; one Friday at three o'clock in the afternoon *Señorita* Estela was ready to return the essays: some of your essays are good, very good and I am very proud of you, it would take a long time to comment on every essay in detail; this is why I suggest you read my remarks attentively; if you have any questions, ask me on Monday; Narcisa did not want to look at her essay before reaching her room; absent-mindedly she walked down Rafael Trejo Street which makes its way behind the church and she was surprised to recognize the door of her house as she could not remember the route she had taken to get there; she ignored the snack of bread and guava preserves Manengo and Florita-Ita were eating at that moment; while she walked up the stairs she felt her heart beating faster, cold sweat was running down her temples, she sat down on the bed, opened the notebook in which she had copied her essay, recognized *Señorita* Estela's handwriting which she had seen so many times on the blackboard, started reading: Narcisa, I did not ask you

112

for a hagiography but for a simple essay; I will quote for you a few passages from Dorita Mitjans' essay that you will admire for their simplicity and clarity: my family consists of Mommy, Daddy and three little brothers who are at school as I am; Daddy works at Cayoguán with a mineral called chrome; Mommy works too, because she looks after us, she prepares our bath and our food; we go to Mass frequently; when somebody has a birthday happiness reigns in the whole family and we are also very happy on Epiphany day and on Christmas Eve and on New Year's Eve, that night we are allowed to wait up for the new year and then we eat the twelve grapes; all right, Narcisa, this will give you an idea of what you should have written, what you say is impossible to understand and has nothing to do with the daily life of a family, for this reason I give you 70%, your teacher, Estela; Note: I do not give you a lower mark because I can see that you have made an effort and I take this into account, your teacher, Estela; on the next day, Saturday, Doña Flora and the children went to the matinée at the Encanto Cinema; after buying the tickets Doña Flora stopped to look at the posters, photographs of scenes from *Spellbound* with Ingrid Bergman and Gregory Peck and in the anticipation of the film she felt the same pleasure she had experienced so often before the radio serials; on Sunday Manengo got up late, he went to the dining room to have breakfast, Doña Flora stayed to drink a cup of coffee with him, she was in a mood to share her feelings with him: imagine those actors who've never been in the movies or if they have

113

I've never heard about them and from one day to the next they get so famous, but you must admit they do make a pretty couple and at the end when she finally decides to stay with him, Lord, it was so good of her to forgive him all those scratches he had made on the tablecloth with his fork, I bet even if the tablecloth was from La Francia he'd have scratched it up with his fork; Doña Flora spoke with animation, taking advantage of one of the rare opportunities she had to talk with her son and she noticed that Manengo's energy was concentrated in his jaws, in that strange forceful way he had of masticating water crackers: well my son, don't you think the end was lovely? don't you think she was right to forgive him •for making those scratches? Manengo pushed away his cup of *café con leche*, placed the rest of his cracker on the tablecloth as if to free himself from the act of eating, spoke with a harshness that Doña Flora would have liked to soften: Mama, didn't you realize all that was only a desperate attempt to identify the place within ourselves where our sense of guilt lives, that guilt which can devour us all at any time? didn't you see that the accidental death of his brother who had fallen over the iron fence and been impaled on the bars had filled that man with such a sense of guilt that it might have driven him to madness? didn't you understand how it is possible to feel guilty simply for being alive while others are dying? didn't you see the connection between the lines he scratched on the tablecloth and the iron bars that had caused the child's death? didn't you realize that the scenography

114

interpreting his dreams was the work of Dali? didn't you realize that the director of the film was Alfred Hitchcock? why don't you read at least a few pages of Freud? why have you been going to the movies all these years? what good has it done you to see Chaplin, Greta Garbo, Douglas Fairbanks Jr., Douglas Fairbanks Sr., Libertad Lamarque, Lillian Gish, Emilio Tuero, Deanna Durbin, Shirley Temple, the Three Stooges, Joan Crawford, Ricardo Montalbán? can't you see how they make the ghosts that live on earth visible by bringing them to the screen? can't you see that they provide us with a vision of our inner being and of our universe? tell me Mama, why do you go to the movies? Manengo left the table and went to lock himself up in his room; Doña Flora kept thinking about that fuss Manengo had made about such a simple film about a woman doctor who was so good and tolerant, you must admit she was very tolerant about that business of the tablecloths and now he wants me to read Froi, Froi and I've heard that man even talks about filthy things and I don't understand how Pascual can allow such books around here and if Father Alvarez knew about this, I'm sure those books are all prohibited by the Church, but what Manengo's saying reveals a lot about him, what he's telling me in fact is that he's going to be a perfect bum when he grows up, because the day Pascual was so proud and happy to tell him: my son, if things continue going so well I'll probably keep working at the Health Department till I retire, because for a while I thought I'd have to quit, but no, they're keeping me and if this goes on I'll work there till retirement and I've been thinking that in six or seven years you could get a job at the Health Department too, I'll start getting the ground ready so they'll give you a little job for a start; and Manengo said something you'd never imagine: I'll never shut myself up in your mediocrity, I must devote my life to the world of the cinema, I'll be a director, a scriptwriter or anything, but I will never be a part of your stupid world; that day I remember Manengo was talking as if he was the master of the house and he went to his room the same as today and poor Pascual just stood here and called him a loafer, a hopeless loafer, that's what you think you're going to be, but don't think you are going to live at my expense when you grow up, if you don't want to work when you are a man you just clear out of here; well, poor Pascual was so angry he dashed out to the café to calm down with a few drinks and so I couldn't say anything to him, because he did need a drink or two if not more, Lord, and who wouldn't if his only son is going to be a loafer and what he said today confirms it, that's what he wants to be and even worse, with that business of Froi or whatever his name is, you can see he's not only a loafer but also a pervert; Doña Flora remained seated, her elbows on the table, her head on her fists; she tried to meditate on the scene with Manengo but her thoughts escaped her and she started thinking about preparing lunch; Narcisa came skipping into the dining room; she stopped on the other side of the table, across from Mama; she fondled the table in little strokes of her right hand; she brought with

116

her that joyous energy she could transmit to cheer up the depressed: Mama, I was in my room and I suddenly knew you weren't feeling well and that you needed me here with you, well, what's the matter? why are you sad on such a nice day when you look so lovely? do you really think you have reasons to be sad? look Mama, you have a husband and children who adore you and this is because you are the queen of this house; Doña Flora spoke to Narcisa with a gesture indicating that she was mistaken and she corrected her: no, Narcisa, I'm not sad, I was just thinking about the *bacanes*, I've almost finished making the fricassee, as soon as it's ready help me chop up the chicken for the stuffing; for the time being let's peel those green bananas to make the dough; after that we'll put the chicken stuffing into little pockets of dough and we'll wrap plantain leaves around each pocket; Narcisa took up the suggestion with enthusiasm and readiness; as soon as everything was ready they started shaping the *bacanes*: they flattened out the plantain leaves on the kitchen table, over that they put a layer of green banana dough, one spoonful of chopped chicken, another layer of dough and finally wrapped the stuffed *bacán* into a plantain leaf; they counted a total of eighteen *bacanes* and put them into a pot of water to boil; Narcisa stood near the pot to watch the water boiling; her eyes shining, she spoke to her mother who was busy washing up some kitchen utensils: Mama, isn't it wonderful to think that a soul could come out of that water passing through the *bacanes* and make them into manna, into nourishment for our blood? well, I don't see who would get himself into a pot of boiling water, certainly not me, and I don't like the idea of my blood boiling like that; Narcisa wanted to retain the light in her round eyes but she felt the astonishment growing in them; Doña Flora remained alone in the kitchen pouring Farola on the scouring pads to get the grease off the pots and pans: it's awful really, that business of having children and that sacrifice of bringing them up, when it's not the flu it's struggling to find money for school and after all that you can't even talk to them because those two, nobody can understand what they say; if it weren't for Florita-Ita I don't know where I'd be; and saying this she felt an urge to confirm what she had just thought; she left the dishes, went to look for Florita-Ita, found her on the sofa with a copy of *Vanidades* open at the page for children's fashions; she went over to her daughter, sat down next to her; Florita-Ita quickly showed her: look Mama, this is the dress I like, I'd like it in white *nansú* with embroidered pale blue flowers with the petals left loose, that girl with the dress looks about six years old and I'm only four, but I know I'm going to look nice in it, I want it soon; Florita-Ita jumped down from the sofa and left the room; Doña Flora kept looking at the open page with the picture of the girl in the dress, thinking of the best way she could get the money together, for although sometimes you can buy remnants of material cheaply, that Candita charges so much it's unbelievable, good Lord, and she's not even one of those fashionable seamstresses like the ones in Havana; in the middle of

118

the academic year Margarita arrived in Narcisa's class; Narcisa had not seen her since the days of Domitila Prieto's school; to Narcisa she seemed more carefree, more self-confident; during recess boys and girls surrounded Margarita to hear her speak about her long stay in Canada, about the months she had spent in Montreal, in Toronto, about that fantastic experience of seeing Niagara Falls; Narcisa walked over to the group, nobody took any notice of her presence; Narcisa felt immensely lonely; a loneliness that took her to a space of rarefied air, she struggled to breathe, she refused to accept this death by asphyxia and this desertion, every one had deserted her, she breathed deeply, I must save myself, I must save myself from the solitude of desertion, I scream, I roar like thunder, I want to find the words that will bring them to the center of my being, it is not yet time for me to die, I scream: this has nothing to do with the journey, but in my grandfather's farm there were guava trees and my Mama says that she made guava preserves herself and that Papa showed her how to make the guava preserves in syrup, but what my Papa knows best is how to make orange peel preserves in syrup, he's an expert, a real expert, he still makes them and they're delicious with cream cheese; heads had turned towards Narcisa, as if compelled by the sound she had forced upon them, drowning the story about Niagara Falls; a few seconds later recess was over; the pupils were about to return to the classroom; Margarita made her way to Narcisa, she looked at her squarely and said to her: it's not the contents of what you say that

119

made them turn their heads, but the noise, that huge noise of your voice; Narcisa watched Margarita go away, followed by the others, she felt the astonishment in her round eyes, she thought that astonishment always overcame her like an act of solitude; that night Narcisa's dreams were filled with blue horses, delicate and graceful, with transparent hides; she saw them ride through the night, they were the only light in the darkness, their light was bluish; once in a while the horses turned their heads and invited her to follow them, especially one horse less transparent than the others which became steely blue and insisted, insisted with the same gestures, trying to tell her something; Narcisa saw herself becoming transparent, she opened her arms to soar into flight but she could not move; she looked towards them, she spoke silently: my time has not yet come, the four pillars in our clan are calling my name; there they are at the bottom of the abyss, they clamor for me, they fill their mouths with pieces of my skin; do not forsake me completely, we shall meet again at another station, do not remove me from the orbit of your journey; Narcisa watched the blue lights rising up into space; on the mattress she felt the weight of her material being; she was sweating profusely; she could not resign herself to the fact that she was awake in a concrete world of compact atoms, atoms that were pressed together and formed a hard crust; she felt thirst and a dryness in her mouth; without wishing to, she got up, went down the stairs, filled a glass with water, sat down at the dining room table, placed the glass before her and looked at it abstractedly without seeing it, turned her eyes away from it towards a corner of the wall; she raised her foot quickly; with her right hand she took off her slipper but she decided to kill the cockroach by catching it and squashing it with her hands; she was filled with pride at this feat and she swore to herself that she would kill cockroaches with her hands to the end of her days; she walked up to the garbage can; she scraped off on the edge of the can what remained of wings and legs, returned to the table to look at the glass of water, meditated as though the act of contemplation would eliminate the necessity of drinking the transparent liquid; time slipped by until Narcisa sensed the break of day, it was almost morning; a chirping sound woke her out of her trance, she thought it was the voice of birds pulling her out of her half-sleep but she realized that the bird voices came from Manengo's room; she pulled the chair away from the table, went to her brother's room, walked in without knocking; Manengo is leaning over a wooden box covered with a blood-stained piece of oilcloth; on the oilcloth there is a rat lying on its back, its body split open; Manengo is still holding the open knife in his hand; he did not protest when he saw Narcisa, for he needed to air some complaints: I had such trouble catching this rat alive and tying it up on this box and now I can't even see how its insides work, I dug my knife in too deep and it died before I had time to examine it alive, pumping blood, even the young it had inside died under the knife, what a savage I am, a real savage, this could have been a phenomenal accomplishment, look my sister, untie the rat, wrap it up in newspapers, put it in a paper bag and go and throw it out two streets away from here and wash the oilcloth for me as I shall need it for other experiments; Narcisa obeyed; while Manengo washed his hands in the bathroom she untied the rat, wrapped it up in newspapers, put it in a paper bag; after Manengo came out of the bathroom Narcisa went in to wash the oilcloth; she walked back to her brother's room, placed the moist cloth over the box and left the room with the paper bag in her hand; when she opened the door to the street the dawn still bore traces of night, she was afraid of walking through the deserted streets; she quickened her step, started running, imagining the dead rat with the young in its belly swinging inside the paper bag, she thought of beginning a litany to hasten the coming of daylight but she only said: I am going to make it, I must make it, everything will be all right; running, she reached the corner of Maceo and Tenth of October streets, she crossed the street and came to the second corner, there she dropped the bag, it flew off, propelled by the momentum of running, and fell heavily on the sidewalk; the return trip seemed easier; when she reached the door which she had left half open she said again: I made it, I knew everything would be all right; she closed the door carefully so as not to make any noise, Manengo's room was closed and she did not dare knock; she climbed up the stairs thinking that achievement, triumph over fear, is a solitary act; Narcisa's ninth birthday passed without any celebration, for Mama owed money to Candita for the last dress she had made for Florita-Ita and the little girl had insisted on Mama buying her a pair of white braided leather sandals she had seen in the window of the shoe store La Perla; Mama had been pinching pennies trying to get enough money together for the sandals and they had not been able to afford to see *For Whom the Bell Tolls*, with Ingrid Bergman and Gary Cooper, and I do wish I could have seen that one, Manengo says it is based on a work by Hemingway, Manengo knows everything and he shouted at Mama: I am fed up with Florita-Ita and her idiotic nonsense, how can you let yourself be dominated by a five-year-old moron? do you think it's logical that we should give up a movie like that for this fool Florita-Ita? Mama was furious and she too was shouting: and who asked you for your opinion, you insolent boy? all you think about is being a parasite with those ideas of yours of becoming a movie director, director, indeed; a freak, that's what you are, a freak; don't you think I know what happened in the school yard with Enriquito? I played dumb because if your father hears about this he's going to beat you up, but don't think I didn't understand Pancha's insinuations, she told me everything even though she did not say anything clearly; aren't you ashamed of yourself? Enriquito is younger than you are; yes, I know, don't yell at me, I know you are only a couple of months older than Enriquito, but what about Gabrielito, Gabriel Pintado's son, he's only eight years old and you're eleven and almost a man, aren't you ashamed, aren't you

123

ashamed? do you think I don't know about Gabrielito? Narcisa remembered her mother seizing a frying pan and making a move to throw it at her brother; she remembered Manengo walking to his room, a feeling of tedium visible on his face, and wanting to be independent, to go away; Narcisa pushed back the memory of the scene, she tried to modify it but it was impossible, she was unable to change it into something delicate and beautiful; she decided to re-invent it by repeating to herself: Mama is a wonderful person, she takes such good care of her children, she does so much for us; Narcisa tried not to think of *For Whom the Bell Tolls* or of her birthday, for it would have been impossible for her to live with herself if she had caught herself criticizing Mama; that evening Don Pascual arrived early; he went up to Narcisa in the living room as though he were expecting something from her; his daughter sensed this, she asks: how was it Papa, were the women after you today? Don Pascual's face expressed pleasure: well, my daughter, those women are really something, all they have to do is wink and I come running, I have to go out tonight, you do understand how it is, don't you? if you were a man you'd be like me, you wouldn't miss an opportunity and you wouldn't be able to keep away from any woman who came near you; Don Pascual smiled happily at the idea of having a child to whom he could transmit his seducer's gift; when he looked at Narcisa he felt close to her, but he also felt there was something missing in her; Narcisa was a little perplexed, she did not quite know what she would have done with that gift, but after a while she thought, why not, Papa is right, those women are really something, take Margarita, I am sure Margarita is really something, I am sure Margarita would love to be seduced; that night after dinner Don Pascual went out as he had said he would, hardly giving Doña Flora any explanation; Manengo went to his room, holding a picture of Gabrielito in his pocket; Doña Flora was thumbing through *Vanidades*, looking for something interesting about her favorite stars; Florita-Ita insisted on being sent to La Inmaculada school when she would be six; Narcisa kept thinking that women were really something; that night Narcisa experienced several hours of profound meditation, she thought of the transitory condition of our being, of the ephemeral quality of our voice, she thought that if matter does not disappear but only changes shape, through changing it becomes another thing, something different from what it was before and we must admit that if matter does not disappear, its original shape nevertheless vanishes; the eternal aspect of things is precisely their transitoriness; in the course of centuries a building becomes dust but in that dust abides transitoriness, dust changes into something else and later into yet another thing; the echo of a voice may persist in the written word in spite of some editorial changes made by hands alien to its essence, but there may be words which are saved entirely and passed on without any change across centuries and this is what I shall be, I shall be the word that carries man to unknown spheres, crowds will follow me, the ethereal weight of my light will descend upon them; I want to anticipate the passage of time, disintegrate, transport my body to the year 2000, look at the world that will be mine at that point in time when I shall have already lived for sixty years; Narcisa felt the weight of her body flying off, detaching itself from her being, fragment by fragment; she felt transparent, she lost consciousness of time and place; all of a sudden she was in Maceo Street, standing before the door of a condemned building that she recognized as her house; her ethereal body made its way through the door; she walked around the empty house in which there were still a few dust-covered pieces of furniture; in the kitchen she recognized the sink where so often Mama had washed the lunch dishes, the breakfast dishes, the dishes for every meal; in a corner there was a copy of *Vanidades* open at a page on Libertad Lamarque, describing her latest triumphs as an actress and as a singer, several pictures of the actress were spread across the yellowish, moth-eaten page; in what had been the dining room she recognized the hammer Papa had used to nail down the patio fence; in a crack inside the dilapidated drawer in Manengo's room she discovered the remains of a time-worn photograph of Enriquito as a child; on the upper shelf of an abandoned wardrobe in Mama's room, a pair of white leather sandals that Florita-Ita had worn when she was five years old and that Mama had kept, hoping to swop them for a larger size or for some piece of clothing with another Mama, because Florita-Ita hardly wore her shoes out and they

126

still looked almost new; Narcisa looked in the dust for other familiar signs; she stood a while before the extinguished masonry coal range; she reconstructed a voice, it was Mama's voice on the day she had helped her make the *bacanes*: look Narcisa, first you put one spoonful of banana paste, then the chopped chicken, then another spoonful of paste, then you wrap it all up in a plantain leaf, yes, please help me count them while we put them into the pot, that's it, I also counted 18 *bacanes*; I'll serve what's left over from lunch with whatever there is and this way I won't have to worry about dinner; Narcisa paced on, searching for traces; where were the people who had lived in the house? Narcisa went up to her room, there she remembered the crib where she had spent her babyhood waiting; she activated her memory and the crib became real, there was the child she had been, she could talk to her; she saw molecules flying, she saw them piling up together at the spot in the room where Narcisa had conjured them; she saw the child clutching the bars, wearing a little shirt and a diaper in which the urine of several days had accumulated; she spoke to her: tell me child, had you ever thought you would reach my age? did you ever imagine yourself in this sixty-year-old skin? tell me child, how did you picture me from your crib? how did you picture me in the year 2000? the child looked at Narcisa: I never imagined you from my crib, but how can you speak of maturity when it is only now you are starting to become a woman? at that moment Narcisa visualized her adolescence, she saw her juvenile cotton skirt thickly sprinkled with little flowers, she saw the flounce at the bottom of the skirt, she saw her linen blouse; she wanted to speak to the girl, but why do I live in this adolescent skin if so many years have passed? the question was not formulated, the girl quickly made herself disintegrate, she quickly disintegrated the crib, both disappeared in a whirlwind of intertwined atoms; Narcisa went to the door of her room, walked across the hallway, climbed down three steps, stopped and looked at the house from upstairs; for a long time she looked down at the dining room, she waited, something was going to happen, something had to happen; suddenly she saw Mama and Papa, they had become old, they were transparent like her; Papa was holding Mama by the arm, Mama was leaning on a stick, she was bent by arthritis; she realized that Mama was speaking: well, come here Pascual, how long are we going to keep doing this? I've been on this side for ten years, I waited for you for one whole year but you took such a long time coming and since you've been here it's the same thing, always the same thing, let's go around the house, but tell me, what is it you are looking for around here? if only we could still visit Manengo and Florita-Ita, Manengo finally got where he wanted to be with those movies of his and he's in Europe, we've always said so, do you remember, Pascual, how we were always telling him, follow your inclination my son, with that talent of yours you are going to succeed; Narcisa thought she was about to hear the crying and the little laugh she had heard so often, but Mama went on: and our Florita-Ita, she's got this talent for declaiming poetry, even now at fifty-six she's better than Paulina Singerman ever was; do you remember those pictures of the children that Florita-Ita sent us? how I'd have loved to meet those children! Pascual, do you remember how I told you some day they'll come and see us and I wonder if we'll understand them when they speak to us in Argentinian, just imagine Florita-Ita going to Buenos Aires with her husband, you know, there's nobody like her and Manengo to think up such ideas! Narcisa saw the old woman repeatedly striking the ground with her stick, well Pascual, are you just going to stand here and do nothing? are we going to be poking around this dust again? tell me, what do you think is going to come out of the dust? Narcisa saw the old man's immutable face, she saw him clenching his teeth and unsuccessfully trying to control the welling up of a tear that rolled down his right cheek; Narcisa went down the stairs, called them aloud, she thought she had shouted, but she saw the old people turn around and move slowly away from her while the old woman kept asking: tell me, Pascual, why did we come here? it's true Manengo and Florita-Ita can't hear us, but who could hear us here? tell me, who could hear us and whom could we hear in this dust? Narcisa saw their transparent bodies go through the walls and disappear; she felt herself moving across time and returning to the present, to this moment in 1949, her atoms flew together to form her body, they clustered down on the bed Chebo had made; at the Colegio Cervantes the academic year was taking its course as expected; during her moments of profound meditation Narcisa wondered how she could live up to the limits of her vision, which extended far beyond the narrow classroom, beyond Maceo Street, beyond the plain of the Yunque, beyond the restless Toa; she thought, I must live through those ages of the earth which have assumed different names in the course of time; she thought, I shall become word and penetrate the earth, I shall inhabit empty spaces devoid of substance; and she would emerge, emerge, bringing forth a philosophy that must rule the universe and penetrate the skin of wanderers whose innocent weight crushes the blades of grass; but what you do not know, Narcisa, is that a community of flesh and blood is waiting to welcome you, let your voice merge into our history, let your image graze the scars in our bodies; Narcisa carried the weight of her books at the end of the leather strap; she watched the trajectory of atoms in the concrete of the pavement; she thought it would take a long time for her words to ripen in the entrails of the earth and in a moment of profound meditation she thought that the time had now come for her to load a tangible masterpiece on the shoulders of the centuries, an eternally transitory creation, a creation that would expand from the short distance of her hand; in a flash she had a vision of Don Carmelo; by a voluntary act of her shoelaces her steps turned towards a shop over which every passer-by could read in enormous red letters, as in a ceremonial banner, CARMELO THE BUILDER, and below, in small black letters: "Building

130

Materials"; Narcisa stopped for a long time, she let her eye muscles go over the outline of every letter, she walked to the entrance; she stopped on the threshold, taking shelter under the doorframe; she stood before Emilio Alfonso, a man who now and then had provoked discussions at the café where Papa had set out to prove his manliness: you don't know what you're talking about, Alberto, I've known Emilio for years and I'm sure Alfonso is his last name, not his first name; but Pascual, you're just arguing with me, I know better because my wife is a friend of Don Carmelo's wife and she knows that Emilio Alfonso is a compound name and Martínez is his last name; okay, if you don't believe me, here's Santiago as a witness, come here Santiago, you're witness to what I say, Alfonso is his last name but Alberto keeps telling me it's his first name and Santiago you're witness that we've bet one peso till Saturday, we'll see which one of us is right; but Narcisa knew they would never check up the information on Emilio Alfonso and that the peso they had bet would remain in Don Pascual's pocket and in Alberto's pocket for months and years; Narcisa studied the bony profile of the clerk who was busily sorting out nuts and bolts which he took out of enormous bags, put into little black boxes and stacked up on one of the shelves along the wall; Narcisa walked over to the counter, she saw him cleaving space as the law of motion required; it occurred to her that Emilio Alfonso was certainly a compound name, a name chosen to describe the bony face of that man who handled the nuts and bolts, chosen to describe his thin

131

hooked nose and the protuberance of his Adam's apple; Narcisa turned down the volume of her voice and made it soft: hello, Emilio Alfonso, yes, I'm Don Pascual's daughter, no, I'm not cutting school, they just let us out early, well, I don't know why, the teacher didn't give any explanation, listen, I should like to speak with Don Carmelo, no, don't tell him Papa sent me but tell him it's urgent, that I absolutely must see him today; Emilio Alfonso's tall bony figure vanished through the opening of an inner door and returned a few minutes later, the nod he gave Narcisa made the command lose its sharpness and become a concession: come in; Narcisa walked to the other side of the counter, Emilio Alfonso had opened a passage for her by lifting a hinged board that served as a bridge; Narcisa walked through the opening of the inner door and found herself in a small room which two desks and a large quantity of paper identified as an office; Don Carmelo was sitting on a round chair; Narcisa noted his huge belly hanging over his thighs, she saw the enormous swelling of the herniated testicles resting softly in the left leg of his pants; Narcisa gauged the manner, she judged the level on which she should speak to Don Carmelo: how are you, Don Carmelo, yes, Mama is fine, Papa too; Narcisa pretended to be interested in the open books, pages filled with numbers in black and red ink: yes, Don Carmelo, I know that you have to do the bookkeeping, balance accounts, tell me Don Carmelo, is it difficult to balance accounts? Don Carmelo pulled the end of the large moustache poised on his upper lip like a huge

132

brown butterfly; he started talking about corporations, bank transactions, porcelain toilets, portable showers, the profound secrets and the mysterious art of masonry, about the molds used to make bricks: look Narcisa, making bricks is a craft hardly anybody knows anything about and maybe some day I'll take you to see the molds, maybe some day there'll be walls in this town that will conceal within them bricks made by your hands; immediately Narcisa was overcome with fascination: you know, Don Carmelo, you are such an interesting person, what do you mean, Don Carmelo, who ever said you were not a loveable man? remember you must not pay any attention to what people say; what is important is knowing that in every brick there is a load of eternal transitoriness; what is important is knowing that in our hands there is an energy that gives a shape, yes, Don Carmelo, a shape we present as an offering to Time in order that it may transform it; Don Carmelo kept looking at the girl who delivered such an incomprehensible speech as she stood on the tiles of the back room which was now his office; the builder tried to explain the strange phenomenon before him: well, no wonder the girl talks like this, her father doesn't just read the paper but also the novels of Vargas Vila and I've heard he's even read *Les Misérables* and the mother knows all that literature on the radio; the butterfly under Don Carmelo's nose twitched and was suddenly restless: tell me, Narcisa, what were you saying about bricks? the ones we have here, well, they've never changed, never, but if you tell me what you mean I'll try to understand what you want; Narcisa walked over to a chair on the other side of the book-laden table and sat down: the fact is, Don Carmelo, there are many things you can do with bricks, this yard is not just full of bricks, it is full of endless creations that will emerge from bricks under the magic of my hands; Narcisa noticed the nervousness of the butterfly trying to understand her words; she spoke more softly: listen Don Carmelo, I should like to play with those bricks, build things with the bricks, I'd like to play an hour or two after school every day, I'll ask for Mama's permission; I'd like to play on Saturdays and Sundays too; Don Carmelo looked reassured, the butterfly became still: but of course Narcisita, you should have said it sooner, I'll tell Emilio Alfonso to have a little pile of bricks ready for you in the yard every day and if you need more I'll give them to you; no Narcisita, don't worry, you don't have to tell me your Papa can't afford any expenses, just come and play and don't worry about the money, just a few bricks my child, that's nothing for me; Narcisa left the back room, walked over to the other side of the counter and to the door, moved through the silence of nuts, bolts and porcelain toilets which was broken by a command: Emilio Alfonso! if Narcisa comes and asks for bricks...; that night Narcisa obtained Papa and Mama's permission to stay after school and work with bricks for a few hours every day; the permission was granted with lack of interest, with apathy; nobody was curious to know what she wanted to do; Manengo was concentrating on the delicate job of

134

mounting a beautiful dead butterfly in a glass case and did not raise his head; Papa was surrounded by a cloud of cigar smoke and went on reading the *Diario La Marina*; Mama said it was the last time she would ever make *bacanes* because this job of wrapping them in plantain leaves, no way, who can stand a job like that, only those who've got a good servant can afford these luxury dishes but those who have to do it all by themselves like me, well, never again, and if anyone wants *bacanes* they had better ask somebody else to make them! Doña Flora went to the kitchen, talking out loud although she knew that at that moment, nobody was listening to her: well, today you're lucky because I spent the whole morning thinking about the Sunday matinée, this Sunday it's going to be *I am a Sinner* with José Mojica and Libertad Lamarque and just thinking about it calmed me down and I stopped being angry about having to wrap *bacanes* in plantain leaves in this heat; the names of Libertad Lamarque and José Mojica soothed Doña Flora like a balm; she was now in an excellent mood, she set the table and served the *bacanes* with pride, almost with joy; Narcisa waited for the moment when she could make her speech on the eternally transitory quality of things, but she had no chance to put in a word and she went to her room and sank into a profound meditation on the act of creation; during the next day in the classroom her isolation was her only companion, she found strength in not letting herself be contaminated by voices, actions, blackboards, books, lessons, papers, notebooks, she devoted herself to a preparatory exercise which she interrupted only twice, thinking that Papa was right, that women are really something and even Margarita would let herself be seduced should she decide to try it; at three in the afternoon Narcisa's brown shoes carried her to the side door of the yard of CARMELO THE BUILDER; Narcisa walked in, using the privilege the owner had granted her; she sized up the materials surrounding her; for the first time she felt centered in her proper environment; in the left corner she recognized the pile of bricks that was meant for her; she walked over to them, with four bricks she built a foundation for a pyre and she repeated the process four times until the monument had reached a height she deemed appropriate; Narcisa climbed up to the top, using other bricks as stepping stones; she spread out her arms and spoke to the universe: from this pedestal I shall reach across the cosmos like a symbol, my work shall be seen everywhere and only the elongated fingers of those who recognize the infinity of my being shall be able to touch it; she lowered her head in profound silence and time was divided into minutes during which Narcisa fell into a trance; she woke up and slowly returned to her earthly dimension, came down from the pedestal, sat down in front of the bricks and meditated profoundly on the destiny her hands would give to the material, she thought of the state of suffocation in which men live and told herself that we bear suffocation on our shoulders like a burden; little by little we feel ourselves dying from it: Narcisa, open for us a window that will

136

let in fresh air, open a window to the sea; Narcisa remained withdrawn within herself in the silence of the afternoon; without attaching any importance to it she noticed that Emilio Alfonso had not brought any mortar; she took two bricks into her hands, stroked them, pressed them together until they formed one whole, infused into her work a form of love that was transformed into energy radiating from the palm of her hands and knew that the bricks had been inseparably joined; this was enough for today; she picked up the leather strap that held her books together and disappeared through the side door of the yard; Narcisa woke up before dawn; during breakfast she was alone with Mama; Doña Flora had woken up in a good mood: listen Narcisa, you know what I dreamed last night? a little black girl with her hair done up in many little tufts came up to me and stuck out her tongue; at first, I tell you, I was angry, because you know it's awfully insulting to stick your tongue out at somebody like that, but then I swear I started laughing and I laughed my head off and I laughed and laughed so much that it woke me up and what about you, did you dream anything last night? Narcisa looked at her vacantly for a while, she was dumbfounded but her astonishment found words: I rode in the desert on a nameless horse and all of a sudden the rain caught me; Doña Flora could not understand the expression on her daughter's face, she felt uncomfortable: well, I don't see why you should make a face like this because you dreamed you rode on a horse; good Lord, if you had seen the peasants

riding horses on your grandfather's farm! and they rode
so easy, Lord, riding a horse looked like the most
natural thing in the world and yours was just a dream,
so that's nothing; Narcisa kept looking vacantly before
her: no, it was not a dream; last night I rode in the desert
on a nameless horse and all of a sudden the rain caught
me; Doña Flora looked at her walking out and thought,
as she had thought several times before, I don't have
much luck really... so much trouble bringing them up
and I can't even have a normal conversation with them;
Narcisa did not allow time to slip by, she controlled it
with her dreams, she appeared distant, lost in a
dimension that nobody could even dream of reaching;
during history class she abandoned her body at her desk
and flew into infinite space to look for answers; that
afternoon while she walked to the yard of the builder
she knew that she had solved the mystery of creation;
she slipped through the opening of the side door and
encountered her raw materials; she took the bricks from
the corner where they waited for her and surrounded
herself with them; she undertook a task that she found
difficult and unspontaneous, she created a shape which,
had it been made of stone, could have been mistaken for
one of those funereal dolmens, for one of those
monoliths assembled at Stonehenge to measure time;
Narcisa looked briefly at the heap of bricks, those few
seconds increased her determination; she demolished
the small monument, she started over; she did not wish
her work to be fated to watch over the dead, she did not
want it to measure seconds, minutes and hours; if she

138

was an infinite being, why should she create something that would symbolize a limitation or a way of measuring things? she took one brick, then another and another still until she had formed a rectangular base from which she built up to the height of her shoulders and even higher, then she had to help herself with a ladder to reach the desired height; Narcisa spent hours at this task which she was achieving by dint of perseverance; she knew, although she would never admit it openly to herself, that the work had had to be forced out of her; she knew, although she would never admit it openly to herself, that it had no purpose or reason for existing; she switched off her inner voice before it could assault her with a truth that Narcisa was not willing to face at that moment; she walked over to the pile of bricks, stroked them for a long time, transmitted to them the warmth of her hands, embraced them, fell into a trance; gradually she woke up and saw that the bricks had been joined together; afternoon changed into evening; Narcisa prepared to go home; she opened the side door but she did not have time to disappear, she was stopped by Don Carmelo's voice: Narcisita, what did you make with those bricks? Narcisa was sorry that she could not keep the secret of her creation to herself for some time at least, but as she gave the explanation she felt impelled by an urge to communicate: it's a chimney, Don Carmelo, it's a tunnel through which the foul air that suffocates us can escape, for only by cleaning ourselves of our impurities can we become free, you might say that this chimney is a window permitting us to reach everything that brings us freedom, don't you think so, Don Carmelo? the builder was shaking his head in a persistent trembling motion which only stopped after he had touched the pile of bricks, then he asked in a hoarse voice at which he was himself astounded: but how is it possible Narcisa, how could you join them together like that, tell me, what did you do to join them? Don Carmelo turned his enormous body to look squarely at Narcisa, but the gap in the door was empty, letting in the night that was beginning to fall; during the meal Narcisa was silent; she made an effort not to hear the pounding of Florita-Ita's demands: look Mama, I'm awfully glad you put me in that school in the middle of the year, you know, at the Inmaculada I'm just like an artist, every five minutes the nuns ask me to give a recitation and though I must wear my uniform during the day, on Sunday afternoon I have to go to the park and wear nice dresses and new shoes because I know the other girls at the Inmaculada have nice clothes and Mama, don't tell me we have no money because Narcisa and Manengo don't need clothes like me and with them you have no expenses; Manengo had finished eating, he threw his napkin across the table and shouted at his younger sister: idiot, you are an idiot, how can you have so little brains, I can already tell what you are going to be later, a moron, an utter moron; Manengo pulled out his chair noisily and walked off to his room; Don Pascual did not scold him for his behavior, for he was also tired of Florita-Ita's demands and as his son's gesture of throwing a napkin seemed manly to him, he did not wish to interrupt such a show of masculinity; Narcisa stayed on after dinner, she did not speak, she observed Mama's worried face, Mama was trying to think how she could solve the problem of the dresses; Narcisa went up to her room silently, she encountered the night, she thought it was time for her to travel to another dimension; she moved her atoms by an act of willpower, she crossed an expanse of space which was heavy and dense with obscurity and dotted with starlight, she soared up to a region where it was still midday, she found herself sitting in a wood near a tree with a slender trunk whose branches had a few leaves left on them, sunlight darted through the empty spaces between the trees, it licked the trunks, it reached Narcisa to warm her; Narcisa allowed herself to rest, she let herself absorb the warmth that caressed her, she closed her eyes and did not let herself sink into meditation, she let time pass without measuring it, she extended her right hand to touch the grass, she felt her fingers stumbling on a metal object which she identified by touch as a tommy gun; she did not wish to disturb her serene mood by asking herself about the purpose and function of the weapon, minutes filed past in a short procession which stopped as Narcisa heard a chafing noise in the grass, a hollow sound suggesting an invasion of bodies crushing the grass; astonished, she opened her eyes and recognized an army of enormous rats about two feet high, it spread before her for yards, perhaps for miles; close to her she could observe their slow heavy movements; the rats did not seem to be

141

aware of her presence; they walked to her left and marched off slowly into infinite space; Narcisa looked at them closely, they had a smooth skin, perfectly smooth and shiny, greyish in color; they appeared swollen, as though about to burst; all of a sudden Narcisa thought she could understand the purpose of the weapon; she placed the tommy gun in shooting position, aimed at a rat coming near one of the slender trunks whose nakedness foreshadowed autumn; she felt the movement of the trigger under her finger, she heard the deafening sound of the shots; she saw blood spouting, as if gushing out of a sprinkler; she saw the empty skin which looked like a deflated bladder; she realized that the rats were only skins filled with blood, they had no bones and no muscles; she could see blood spilled on the reddish soil and from between the lumps of bloodstained earth new rats multiplied and, disregarding the passage of time, grew to the size of the others; she saw them appear and swell the crowd without the slightest hesitation, as if they knew that this was their destiny; Narcisa dropped the weapon, she understood why the rats had been indifferent to the sound of gunshots and to the possibility of death; she quickly let her atoms disintegrate in order to return to her other dimension; she was sitting on her bed again, the clock indicated midnight; at breakfast Manengo was in a hurry, for he had arranged a meeting with Enriquito before school; Florita-Ita was happy with the idea that somehow, thanks to the sacrifices of others, she would get her dresses and her shoes; Don Pascual was eager to leave and buy the newspaper before going to his office at the Health Department; Doña Flora was grumbling about the circumstances that escaped her control: Narcisa, can you see what I'm up against? imagine, I was able to save a *medio* yesterday and I dropped it and it fell down the drain without rhyme or reason; I make so many sacrifices just to save a penny and there it goes, just like that; if I had tried for years to throw it down the drain I probably would have missed, I'm such a bad shot and now it hits the mark all by itself; Narcisa picked up the leather strap with her books that were lying on the floor, she stood before her mother and looked at her: everything has its destiny and it's useless trying to oppose it with our physical strength, for even if we destroy things they will multiply again, they will multiply destiny in the very blood they have shed; Doña Flora dried her hands on her apron, as if seeking support and reassurance for the words that this time she was unable to silence: well, that's not it really, as far as I am concerned, even if I am furious to have lost the *medio*, that doesn't mean I'll start bleeding, I may not like what happened but I won't be shedding blood about it, no way; Doña Flora walked around in the dining room and the kitchen, she was happy she had told Narcisa what she deserved to hear; Narcisa skipped away to the door, she was also happy because her mother had not understood her; that afternoon Papa came home earlier than usual, he was not feeling well, he lay down on the sofa; after returning from the workshop, as she called Don Carmelo's yard, Narcisa found him reading the

143

newspaper, he was still lying on the sofa and his face bore a slight paleness that Narcisa attributed to fatigue from work: how are you Papa, how was it today, tell me about all those women, are you going out tonight? Narcisa's cheerful mention of his favorite subject did not meet with the same welcome as it had at other times, Don Pascual tried to smile at his daughter but he was unable to speak; Narcisa saw him faint, the newspaper fell to the floor, he did not answer when she called him, she ran to the kitchen: Mama, Mama, Manengo, there's something wrong with Papa, run, there's something wrong with Papa; Doña Flora started screaming: mercy, Lord, what's happening, if that man dies on us now, what are we going to do, what shall I do with three children still at school? Florita-Ita got up from the small rocking chair where she was looking at the latest fashions in *Vanidades*, walked to the sofa, looked at Papa who was unconscious and went back to her chair with the magazine; after all, this was a problem for the others to solve; Narcisa knocked violently at her brother's door: Manengo, Manengo, run and fetch Doctor Méndez, it's Papa, I think Papa's had a heart attack, he could die, run Manengo, get Doctor Méndez; Manengo opened the door, he was angry: if you want Doctor Méndez to come you'll have to get him yourself, today I've just received an article on Frank Capra and I won't leave it to run and get anybody; Manengo closed the door; Florita-Ita went on rocking herself and reading the magazine; Doña Flora paced through the house in panic, screaming; Narcisa went up

144

to her: Mama, I'm going to get Doctor Méndez, you stay with Papa, rub his forehead with alcohol; Narcisa ran out and disappeared; the two blocks to the doctor's house seemed endless to her; she knocked desperately at the door and Alfredito, the doctor's eldest son answered; Narcisa's broken and anxious words attracted the attention of Josefina, Doctor Méndez's wife who tried to calm Narcisa down: don't get so upset my child, I'm sure your Papa doesn't have anything serious, no, the doctor isn't here, he went to Moa yesterday and he hasn't come back yet, but don't worry; Narcisa did not let her finish, she ran to Hilario's pharmacy: listen Hilario, it's about my Papa, it could be a heart attack, he's unconscious, give me a bottle of ammonia and please come with me, Doctor Méndez is in Moa, you are a pharmacist, please Hilario; Narcisa ran home, Hilario followed her at a distance; Narcisa walked in through the door which she had left open, went up to her father, opened the bottle of ammonia, made him smell it; Don Pascual gave a start, opened his eyes and coughed: oh Papa, what a fright you gave us, but it's over isn't it, everything is all right isn't it? Don Pascual made a gesture to indicate that he was well, but very tired; Hilario was there, he brought a chair near the sofa; with a doctor's bearing he made his diagnosis in a low voice: listen Pascual, at your age you should calm down, everybody knows there's not a woman who can come near you without you... the two men seemed to enjoy the subject of Don Pascual's extraordinary virility; Doña Flora had relaxed enough to bring Hilario a cup of

145

coffee, he drank it with the satisfaction of having earned it with his diagnostician's powers; he went back to the pharmacy, thinking that if he was not a doctor he was no pharmacist either, for he had bought the pharmacy with his wife's inheritance and that didn't make him a pharmacist, but if he only could have studied he would have been a real genius, he had the stuff of a doctor in him and nobody could deny it, all he had had to do was to come near Don Pascual and he had him cured on the spot, how talented he was; Hilario stood behind the counter until a customer broke off his broad smile: listen Hilario, I've had a toothache for three days and I can't even sleep; Hilario turned around, leaned over to search through the lower shelves; the woman could see his black hair turning grey at the temples, it occurred to her that Hilario must be about forty-two years old; she thought, what would we do in this town without this man who can cure everybody, and her idea was confirmed as she heard him say: listen Rosalía, take this bottle of iodine and apply some to your tooth with cotton wool three times a day, if in two days you still have pain I'll give you some sulfa powder; if the pain doesn't stop with the sulfa then it's probably not an infection but a cavity and you'll have to go to a dentist; the customer left thinking that having Hilario in town was definitely a godsend; Narcisa went back to the workshop and found her chimney as she had left it, but there were no bricks in the usual corner; she quickly surveyed the situation, looked around, went up to the piles of bricks scattered about the yard; she applied

146

herself to the task of choosing some bricks and piling them up carefully in the corner where she was used to working; she noticed that her work was becoming increasingly difficult, less spontaneous, slower; she knew it would take her several days to finish each chimney, she knew that an indissoluble relationship had been formed between the work and herself; during the course of the next few days three or four chimneys were built; Narcisa aligned them without touching them, moving them with the energy that radiated from her fingers as soon as she came near each completed work; she placed her hands about an inch away, her fingers spread out like a star, she transmitted to them the motive force that conveyed each monument to the position Narcisa had assigned it against the wall of the yard; they could have been a row of red pines or red cypresses watching over the yard and waiting for the accomplishment of their destiny; Narcisa felt penetrated, filled with that force of creation that was becoming a part of her nature; at one precise point in her history she realized that there was no more space within her, so she tried to extend the space into her brother: Manengo, my brother, you must see my work, with whom shall I share this unless it be with you? I cannot go on any longer, this is too much for me, I must share it with you; Manengo received Narcisa's enthusiasm coolly; he did not feel like being bored to death walking to the builder's yard and looking at some old piles of bricks, but he had to please Narcisa at least once, if only this one time, for if Narcisa became tired of his demands, on whom would he be able to rely in his family? all right Narcisa, we'll go together tomorrow after school; Manengo's black shoes, Narcisa's light brown shoes reached the builder's yard; Narcisa could hardly breathe, she knew that she had to slow down the working of her lungs so that her breathing could support the ecstasy that was filling her; she studied her brother's face, waiting for the moment when he would be touched by the magic of her work, but at that moment Manengo was conjuring up a vision of Enriquito giving up the idea of waiting for him at the Fire Brigade barracks from which they had arranged to go together to the house of Angelita, Enriquito's godmother; there they would have spent a few hours alone together, the godmother would return from Victoria de las Tunas that night; every day during the week she had been absent Enriquito had gone over to the house to see if everything was in order, just as his godmother had told him; Narcisa was a little impatient at her brother's lack of interest: well, tell me, what do you think? Manengo pursed his lips into a wrinkled circle: well, it looks like a waste of time, energy and materials; Narcisa saw him walk to the door hurriedly, then disappear; she remained motionless in the yard and told herself that Manengo had spoken like that so the perfection he had seen in her work would not make her conceited, for conceit leads to a paralyzing idleness and only brings us to a pointless contemplation of our own work; Narcisa stood before the row of chimneys that leaned against the wall of the yard; she spread out her arms: at this moment, while the

148

sun radiates its light over the earth, I must thank my brother for the influence of his wisdom on my work; you who are the product of my hands have been shaped thanks to the stroke of inspiration he instilled in me; together, you and I, we form a unit that has become compact and indissoluble, thanks to the power and the grace of the Crowned One; after her prayer there was a long silence during which the chimneys appeared majestic, attentive, as though trying to understand; on the way to Maceo and Tenth of October streets Narcisa was seized with an infinite love for her brother and her state of ecstasy was broken only by the proximity of the door knocker, of the front door, of the facade of what she recognized as her house; she went in, walked to her room; she had to preserve in silence an experience such as today's; she sat down on the bed, leaned against the headboard and sank into profound meditation, telling herself once again that her brother was the supreme guide of her work; although she made no special effort to measure time, Narcisa realized that she had waited for dinner longer than usual, she decided to go down to the living room, she found her mother next to the radio, interested in an episode of *The Errant Avenger*; she sensed that her brother was in his room behind the locked door; she heard Florita-Ita talking to herself, throwing into the air demands that someone buy her a latex bathing suit with blue and white stripes, like the one her friend from La Inmaculada had bought at Fin de Siglo; Papa had not yet come home; Narcisa started setting the table; she had set three places as the sound of

149

the key in the latch told her that Papa was coming in; she was about to ask him about his conquests of the day, but Papa's violent expression kept her silent; Don Pascual took off his jacket and threw it on the sofa, forgetting how often he had heard Doña Flora complain that she was tired of picking it up; he walked to his son's room, knocked repeatedly and without even waiting a few seconds, kicked the door several times until Manengo opened reluctantly; the door remained open and from every part of the house they could hear ragged fragments of his voice: Angelita's neighbors, you wretch, seen from the roof garden, if you now start playing your pansy games right in Angelita's yard, going to rip out your guts, you queer, imagine having a son like this, the worst shame, you're not a real man, going to bash your face, better control myself; Don Pascual slammed the door, went into the bathroom, shouted for a towel; Doña Flora brought him the change of underclothes he had not asked for, a clean towel, a shirt and a pair of pants; she walked aimlessly, silently around the house; Narcisa thought her brother would not be able to eat anything that night; she imagined him haggard, ashamed, indignant; she started devising solutions, with cinematographic speed she saw herself putting aside some of her food for him and bringing it to him secretly and she would tell him that she understood him and accepted him and that no one had a right to interfere with his sexual preference, for after all homosexuality is frequent in Greek mythology and even if it's not it should be, because the gods are multi-sexual

150

and if they are, why shouldn't we be? Narcisa was about to pursue her imaginary dialogue with her brother, but he came out of his room and sat down at the table where everyone had gathered; she saw him help himself to an enormous portion and eat systematically with pent up voracity; at dessert time she saw him push himself forward and fill his plate with guava halves and cream cheese before anyone else; Don Pascual knew it was useless to continue showing indignation, he let himself be overcome by tiredness and felt suddenly exhausted; Narcisa thought that perhaps her brother could live without her approval, she thought perhaps this wonderful being was sufficient unto himself, perhaps she was not very important in his life; she was in her room, sitting on the bed at the very spot her crib had occupied years before; the door was pushed half open by Manengo: my sister, I must talk to you, it is absolutely necessary that I talk to you; Narcisa's round eyes watched her brother's lips pursed up in a wrinkled circle, he looked as if he were just about to address a few tender words to himself: my sister, you must help me, if you don't who will, tell me, on whom can I depend in this house except on you? Narcisa took her brother's hands between hers and prepared to listen, her mouth half open, her eyes astonished; she felt touched by magic: tell me my brother, tell me what you want, what am I here for if I don't help you? Manengo was now reassured, he began his request: there's going to be a course in cinematography with technical instructors; but Papa, you know I can't count on him, it's going to take place in Evangelina's outbuilding and there's registration, you know artists aren't cut out for work, but you could do it, Papa told me if he talked to someone he could get me a job as a rates collector for water and electricity, I'm going to accept it, but I'd like you to do the work and we'll tell him I'm doing it; Narcisa was filled with tenderness and excitement: my brother, we are here to help each other, I can start tomorrow; Manengo walked out of the room without thanking her and locked himself up in his room; Narcisa started going out in the early hours of the morning to collect the first payments before going to school; she returned home at the time when the others were starting to get up; Narcisa had to work harder, for Manengo's registration was more expensive than the amount she earned from one job, she became a debt collector for two corner grocery stores, a shoe store, and a lottery ticket stand; at her workshop she had to work faster at her creative task, she shaped the materials with voracity in order to organize her work during the little time she had when she could get away from her collector's jobs; one afternoon while she was anxiously working in the yard Don Carmelo came out; he seemed in a bad temper: look Narcisa, when I told you you could use some bricks, I didn't mean you should come every day and use a whole heap and make those things, we hardly have room for all those chimneys, I've tried to demolish all this but it's impossible, you may keep on coming and you may play here as much as you like, but you can't take any more bricks, there's no room for any more of these chimneys; Narcisa leaned over a chimney she had just finished, for a long time she stroked the bricks and with the energy from her hands she guided the chimney, which aligned itself next to the others against the wall; Narcisa left the row of chimneys without a word; she was grateful for the fact that they had sprung from her hands, she was grieved by a separation that seemed final; while she walked to the door she heard Emilio Alfonso's voice, urgent and confidential: don't worry Don Carmelo, tonight there will be a full moon, I'll be here at midnight, the ceremony will be successful, tomorrow all these chimneys will have become bricks again; Narcisa went away imagining Emilio Alfonso in the moonlight, his blade-like figure cutting through the night; she imagined the bricks lying peaceful and powerless on the ground in the workshop; before going home she made her last run for the payments of the day; when she came in everyone was sitting at the table; Papa's unquestioning silence told her that he had discovered everything, he knew that it was really she and not Manengo who went to collect the payments, but at the same time she felt certain that Papa would not do anything about it, so as not to be forced to acknowledge yet another of his son's weaknesses; Narcisa postponed her return to the workshop, she let days pass so that she would not have to face a reality that spelled desolation; her collector's jobs were affecting her, she had rings that looked like greenish black spots under her eyes; sometimes she felt like saying that she too needed time, that while walking through the streets she felt in her

153

hands the urgency to shape her own work; but this way at least, her brother's dream had come true: my brother, haven't you found your way? tell me, which aspect of film-making are you most interested in? she saw her brother recoil suddenly: Narcisa, even if I explain you won't understand anything, maybe I'll start writing scripts, but to be able to do something like that I'll have to understand films from within; Narcisa did not tell him that she did understand, for she too had a need to create that grew from her fingers, but she knew that now was the time for silence and she prepared to settle the accounts that she kept in a paper bag together with a few pesos; she would settle accounts with one of the grocery stores at midday during the lunch break between classes, an hour she had not had free for months; towards the end of the school year Narcisa told herself that she would now have a period of vacation, and rest, a period during which her time would belong to her and to her work, without interference from others and during which she would build a series of chimneys that would leave an indelible mark on the history of creation; there in the workshop the bricks were piled up like cells which had been loosened from the former chimneys; seeing her work destroyed did not devastate her as she had thought it would, but it gave her a new incentive to create, to confirm that the act of creation is indestructible in itself, that the instant of creation remains permanent in time and untouched by the endless course of centuries; the created work may vanish, but the moment of creation becomes an

154

imperturbable and eternal god; that same day Narcisa started experimenting with new designs that seemed to her different from those of her previous chimneys and which were only previews or rough models for what was going to be the column of summer; she sat down on the sofa, her hands resting between her thighs; Florita-Ita was examining some loose pages from what had been a Sears catalogue; Manengo was on his way to his room, he was stopped by Narcisa's voice: come here my brother, I must tell you about my plans for the summer; I am going to start a new row of chimneys, once you see what I am doing you won't believe it, although what I am doing now is only an experiment, a preview of what I am going to do this summer; with no classes and no jobs, just imagine what I will be able to do with my energy, you must come and see what I am doing; Manengo was about to ignore her, but he stopped: of course I'm interested to see what you are doing, but with all the things I have to do I never have time to go to the workshop, though I'm very much interested, very much, the day I went to the workshop I could see you were an artist, a real artist, but my sister, I don't think you can stop working this summer because during those months I'll have to buy books, get information, buy magazines with articles on the cinema and in September I'll carry on taking that special course which is becoming more expensive all the time and you know, this is a calling, a lot more than a simple vocation, for me it is now a way of life; after I've bought the books, put the money you have left over in an account in my name at the bank, you know I depend on you my sister; Narcisa was about to say, that is what we are here for, to help each other, but Manengo left before his sister could start speaking; Florita-Ita called from her small rocking chair: don't think you are going to give all of it to Manengo, you have to buy my clothes for September, Mama told me to ask you and Papa too; I want dresses like the ones in these pictures here, like the ones American girls wear and I won't wear last year's uniform again next fall; suddenly Narcisa felt weak and faint; at ten years of age she felt as if she had fallen into a deep hollow in the tunnel of time and was unable to go on; everything became dark before her eyes, she felt weightless, she thought this might be the coming of death; at the mouth of the tunnel the voices of four monsters shouted her name; she felt the vibrations of their voices pulling her in their direction; she was propelled towards them with the velocity of the Paris pneumatic dispatch system; she emerged through the mouth of the tunnel, she recognized the monsters one by one, she saw them devouring pieces of her skin with both hands; frightened, she opened her eyes; Mama, Papa, Manengo, Florita-Ita, all four of them stood before the sofa with their arms crossed; Mama spoke to her: we were calling you, what happened, did you faint? we kept calling you and you didn't answer; Narcisa sat up, resting her left hand on the back of the sofa, she did not mention the experience of the tunnel, she did not want to say that she would have preferred the voices not to pull her away, that it would have been good not to have to come out, that it would have been good to sail around in infinite space; during the summer she divided her time as best she could, the streets she had once loved now seemed to her dull to the point of loathing, the excuses she was receiving were an endless litany: the mistress isn't here, come back later, Narcisa; it's still too early for collecting, the payment was due just two days ago; I told you only a week ago, you must come at night when my husband is here; look, I won't be able to give you a cent until next month because my brother and his wife are visiting us and with all these expenses we don't have any more money; all I can give you today is five *reales*, the day after tomorrow it's Nenita's birthday and we have to celebrate it; look, here are two pesos and this settles the previous account, don't come for the new one before six weeks from now; with each excuse Narcisa breathed out heavily through her nose; she went away, snorting a little and sucking her lower lip; Narcisa plodded through the summer, she let it go by, she saw it being added to the accumulation of time from past centuries; her work seemed to progress slowly, she had no time to make plans, she had no time to invent new designs or go to the workshop to execute them; Doña Flora devoted herself almost entirely to the episodes of *Tamacún the Errant Avenger*; Papa was more absent than usual, that made Mama shout: are you going out with that tart of a nurse again? she probably thinks you've got money and she wants to get it from you; Papa smiled with some satisfaction at the thought that women were fighting over him, but he had never heard Mama speaking to Tamacún at 7:30 in the evening: he thinks he makes me suffer because he left me alone, well, what a joke, this way I have peace to think about the Avenger, really Tamacún, you look just perfect in that turban of yours, you're not one of those Arabs like Teófilo, the one at the variety stand, there is a certain mystery about you and no one can escape from you, for you know that every criminal has to pay; and then the music played and Mama was silent; during the whole summer Narcisa did what her family expected and when September came she continued to do so; schoolwork took place at a level far removed from magic, it became routine, it's just classes, work, obligations towards others and there is my work, my work is left behind, orphan of my time; Narcisa saw the evening fall, on the way home she knew that her collector's job had delayed her return for dinner, she was fully conscious of her steps crossing the threshold; she heard Mama piling up the plates and the cooking pots for her to wash; she did not pause to eat, she did not stop to ask if they had kept her a plate of food; she started to wash the dishes alone, far away from the others; her tiredness went beyond muscles, bones, and blood cells; she sprinkled Farola on the scouring pad several times to remove the grease from the pots and pans; for plates and glasses she used the piece of yellow Candado soap she had found lying on one of the tiles near the sink; she finished drying the last utensils: a fork and a small spoon; she walked through the house, ignoring Florita-Ita's claims: two girls at the Inmaculada

158

have rings already, look Mama, buy me a little ring, even one from Farit the Arab's variety stand will do, but better one from Isalgué's jewelry store, well, it's all right if it's from the Arab's stand but I'd prefer one from the jewelry store; Narcisa saw lines on Mama's forehead and she could read the question: but where am I going to get the money for rings? it's true that having children..., really, letting Pascual get on top of me and afterwards giving birth to this pack of trouble, that's what children are, trouble that never ends, never-ending trouble; Narcisa wanted to go and console Mama for the trouble she had to go through with her children, but she saw her nervously twisting the buttons of the radio, trying to get the station with the lovely music that announced *The Spirit*, music Mama would never recognize as Dvorak's Ninth Symphony, from the New World; she decided to go to her room and left Mama to a happiness she would never have been able to give her as fully as *The Spirit* or as Tamacún did; while she was climbing up the stairs she noticed that Papa was deep in the *Diario La Marina* and intensely absorbed in the task of smoking an enormous cigar; she sensed Manengo's presence behind his locked door; she reached the hallway, went through the opening to her room, lay down and stretched on the bed that now occupied the spot where her crib used to be; she threw her books on the floor; still wearing her street clothes, she sank into profound meditation; her astral body began moving with a strange undulating rhythm, with a pumping rhythm like that of the heart or the lungs; she made a

159

sudden leap into space, she did not know which points she had touched in the night, she penetrated time, projected herself into it, she explored several decades; she saw the figures of Papa and Mama, still alive, already old; Mama was bent by arthritis and she spoke like a general to Don Pascual who was weakened by old age; she could sense his deterioration, the erosion of time, the devastating effect of arteriosclerosis on Papa; she saw him at eighty-two, he was trying to remember the road between the park and his house; she saw him weep as he realized that his memory was failing him; she saw him weep over and over because recently in a dream he had been told that Doña Flora had been unfaithful to him with his friend Alberto, although it was never clearly revealed whether the adultery had been in her thoughts only or whether it had actually taken place; she saw Don Pascual going repeatedly to his wife and reproaching her: some things really make you sick, some things would make anybody sick; and after the reproaches, the dejected expression and the complaining: imagine that woman doing this to me, imagine that woman soiling my honor like this; Doña Flora was sitting in the armchair, rocking and lamenting: imagine that man making me suffer like this, it's unbelievable, inventing lovers for me in my old age; when Narcisa woke up she heard what sounded like the song of birds at dawn, a dawn she imagined to be glorious; she prepared to get up, thinking: the house I saw was empty, those old people were alone in a house without children; after a few months Narcisa sought a temporary solution, a way of being able to devote herself to her work; she had expanded her collector's jobs to the maximum and slowly she had put together the complete sum well before the time of registration; she counted each payment until she had money for six months in advance; she said nothing about the money hidden away in the silence of her room, so that no emergencies would arise which would devour it with the speed of lightning: magazines with articles by King Vidor, skirts like the ones the friends from the Inmaculada wore; the powder compact that Mama had mentioned daily until Narcisa decided to go by La Perla and came home with a little package: look Mama, here's a little present I bought for you; as the gift was received there was the little laugh and the crying and then a protest: well, it was about time, I've seen this for so long at La Perla and I couldn't afford it, all my life I've made sacrifices and made sacrifices and I could never afford a powder compact no matter how many times I passed by that window, but finally somebody brought me one; even Papa had gotten into the habit of sending her to fetch the newspaper and cigars without giving her the money to pay for them; moreover it was her business to keep herself fitted out with clothes, a necessity which she kept to a minimum; she would now work for two more weeks so that the lottery ticket stands and the water and electricity companies would have time to find a new collector; after that she would spend every day at the workshop and nobody would suspect that she had stopped working; every month she would give Manengo some money for registration, she would tell him that the situation was not good, that business was in a slump, that she had lost customers and for this reason she could not buy him anything more after paying for his registration, and of course Manengo would understand, for this pure and generous being who loves me in such a beautiful way, how could he not understand, indeed his heart is so noble that he keeps nothing for himself, he gives everything away, to tell the truth I am so moved by this strange and extraordinary being who is my brother; Narcisa decided to inaugurate the day of her return to the workshop with a ceremony; she spent a restless day confined at her school desk, nobody could speak to her, nobody was able to draw her out of her abstracted state; when the three o'clock bell rang she quickly left behind classrooms and hallways and went out to the street; wearing a fateful expression she walked to the builder's yard; in the usual corner she piled up several bricks to be used as a pedestal; she climbed up and remained standing, her eyes closed, almost in a trance: here I stand on this pyre, the accumulation of my work always becomes a pyre where the bodies of the dead are burnt, where the victims of sacrifices are turned to ashes, for the sacred fire devours death in order to create windows for breathing; bricks shall arise at the touch of my hands to form a procession of chimneys, of infinite lighthouses that shall spread my light over the Earth; during the next few days silence was Narcisa's only companion; she devoted herself to the business of collecting payments, feeling relief at the idea of her forthcoming liberation; days went by and she reached the deadline she had given herself; Narcisa spent hours in the yard appeasing the hunger of the first encounter; when she came home nobody protested at her being late, nobody asked her if she wanted to eat; all were taking a rest, oblivious to the dishes they had left for Narcisa to wash; in a pot she noticed some left-over boiled plantains and a few bits of what had been shredded meat; Narcisa ate directly from the pots, standing; she was not conscious of the act of eating and she soon finished her frugal meal; she applied herself to washing the dishes, then slipped away to her room so that she would not have to speak; she had to let her work mature in silence; on the second day Narcisa waited for evening among the bricks that were taking the same shape as the previous chimneys which had been joined by Narcisa's fire and separated under the light of the moon by Emilio's magic words; but Narcisa persisted in believing this: these chimneys are different, the fire of my creation is being multiplied and thus an entirely new work will be born, different from the previous one; Narcisa noticed that the zinc awnings on the facade were closing like corrugated eyelids; she quickly left the yard; she walked home in a mixed state of satisfaction and anxiety; at the entrance she unhooked the door catch and went in; the house was unusually lit up; Mama was in the living room, her left leg was swollen, wrapped in bandages and resting on a bench; Mama's voice anticipated her questions: well, it's about time you came, you're lucky I knew you were out there doing your collecting, else I'd scold you for not being here because I slipped and twisted my ankle and now it's all swollen and this happened in such a silly way, just a wrong step, your Papa hadn't come home yet and you know it's impossible to depend on that shameless good-for-nothing brother of yours and if Pancha hadn't come over to bring me a cup of coffee I wouldn't even have been able to send for Hilario who came right away with arnica and bandages and recommended I shouldn't move for a few months and today we managed because Pancha brought us something from her *cantina*, a nice soup and a *cocido* and she made us a potato omelet and that way we had enough, but look, I can't even move; I'll send a message to school so they'll let you out early and you can do the cooking before Papa gets home and you'll have to set the table and mop the floor and wax it every other day and you'll have to do a bit of washing every day because we can't give all the laundry to the washerwoman and now with this thing of mine, synovitis, that's what Hilario calls it, you'll have to stay home and we won't be able to rely on the little money you were making on your collector's job and on top of that we have to get money for your sister's uniform, they are going to put her in the band even though she's little and can't play any instrument, they want her as a mascot; Narcisa washed the dishes in a silence that left a taste of sand on her gums, in her throat, in the canals leading to her stomach; she went to her room, bearing a disappointment too great to allow protest; after she had closed the

164

door, Mama's voice found its way through the cracks: set the clock for six o'clock so you'll have time to make coffee and get breakfast ready; Narcisa sat down on the bed without taking off her clothes; her round eyes were going over visions in the dark; she felt an urge to escape, to find a new formula for breathing; she thought, why not be like Papa: taking women by surprise without thinking of the risk of rejection, this is what women like, that's what Papa says, so if Margarita comes I could take her by surprise and already I can see her before me, her hips and her womanly breasts are growing and night impels me to take her, but this woman becomes diluted, losing her sex among the branches, and I go into the forest for if there were still gnomes there, winter would turn into spring; and we walk touched by magic, weeds of steam rise under our footsteps, but we have come here to conquer, to feel the swift night bristling against our skin; we wander down the paths, we are surrounded by the lonely night mist, you walk on without looking at me, you walk by my side facing the dusk, your voice is dispersed through space, we wander along a deserted field; I see you walking before me, I follow the edge of your shadow, we halt our pace, we halt the pace of migratory clouds, we halt the movement of our skins near the tree of the gnomes, we wait for silence, for yours, for mine, for the silence of air spreading over roots; I see you walking, you refuse your destiny of a disquieting muse, I see you break through the night like an abstract vision; I follow the edge of your shadow, we cross the wood, a path,

165

penumbral fragments, and I keep inventing your steps which become voices among the leaves; there you emerge, you have become so small, you gather yellow flowers among the shadows; solitude dies in the grass as you shower me with yellow flowers; I see you grow larger again as you walk; I follow the edge of your shadow that shall be the edge of my shadow in this desolate field of yellow flowers; Narcisa jumped up at the irritating sound of the alarm clock that indicated six o'clock; she got up without the slightest wish to begin a task that she found unacceptable; she managed to prepare breakfast; when she came to school she gave Mama's note to the teacher: please let my daughter leave school at eleven today for I have synovitis and I am resting according to the prescription of Hilario the pharmacist and my daughter must look after me, for this reason she will stop going to school for some time until I am better, sincerely yours, Doña Flora; at eleven Narcisa got her books together and prepared to leave; Margarita was waiting for her at the door; Narcisa thought that the silence of her eyes held the mystery of the forest and she stopped to look at her briefly and intently before leaving; when she came home she was met by Mama's voice: well my girl, it's about time you came, I'm just dying with thirst, bring me a glass of water; and the voice was multiplied as the day passed: Narcisa, make me a cup of coffee, Narcisa, take me to the bathroom, I've been wanting to go for hours but you don't even think of asking me, Narcisa, you've just finished waxing the dining room floor but you've missed some parts, look at how many dull spots there are on this floor, don't tell me you did it everywhere, I won't believe it; Narcisa, fill the bathtub and help me take a bath, Hilario told me I couldn't move with this synovitis of mine, Narcisa, get me a snack, a cup of *café con leche* but make sure the milk is hot because at breakfast you served it lukewarm and nobody can take it like that and I want some guava paste and bread and cheese, Narcisa, why does it take you so long to wash a few clothes? fortunately Pancha persuaded your Papa to let us order meals from the *cantina* till I could manage, what would we do otherwise, the only thing you have to do is make breakfast and it takes you hours; Narcisa, go to Pancha's house and bring me the collection of Corín Tellado's novels she said she would lend me, Hilario prescribed rest and all I can do is listen to the radio and read novels and that's it, and when you come back get the arnica cataplasms ready, Hilario says it's the only thing that helps against synovitis; on Saturday morning Narcisa went out to do the shopping, for Manengo had refused to be errand boy until such time as Mama could manage to walk; Mama had often clamored for the right not to go to market, just imagine, why should a lady go to the marketplace and walk back across town loaded with parcels like a servant, but of course, Pascual, I should have thought of all this when I married you, because you'd never think of getting me a maid, Lord, even Pancha has somebody who does the dishes and the shopping for her; but Mama's scenes and shouting had never brought a maid into the house and now that Mama

167

is sick we manage by sending one of Palomo's sons to the store once in a while and here is the shopping list, soup meat, noodles, chick peas, rice, *vianda*, starch and a bar of Candado soap; Narcisa put the list in the left pocket of her white blouse; she took her steps without hurrying and walked past the house of their neighbor Pancha; she came to the empty front porch of the next house, no, it was not empty, Glorita was sitting there in the middle of the floor, dressing up paper dolls; Narcisa went up to the railing: hello, aren't you the new neighbor who just moved to the district, aren't you the daughter of the notary from Bayamo? ah, you're going to go to the Inmaculada? well, if you had gone to Cervantes they might have put you in the same grade with me, I'm so glad you've moved here, me, I'm just doing some shopping because Mama isn't well and the maid couldn't come today, wait till you know my Mama, she's wonderful, my Mama is so nice, so adorable, she's a honey and my Papa's a honey too, and my brother is going to be a movie director and my younger sister declaims poetry and I want you to come and see my work, when you see it you won't believe it, no, you have to come with me because as I said to my friends at school, you are all trying to shine for a span of time during which you'll do nothing important, but as for me, I create for posterity; you know, Glorita, I think you're awfully nice and that's why I'm telling you you should see my work, why don't we go right away? Glorita had frowned a little as if to protect herself against the booming voice that insisted, let's go, let's go immediately, but she slowly abandoned her paper dolls on the floor; she announced from the door, which was held open with a catch: Mama, I'll be back right away, I'm just going to the corner with the girl next door; Narcisa went on in her deafening roar: I'm just finishing a collection that's worthy of a museum, it has a quality which artists from this town have never been able to achieve, nor have artists from other towns, even those from France and when you see my work then you will tell me which artist from the Renaissance has created anything like that; Glorita followed Narcisa to the builder's yard and walked to the row of chimneys that rested uncomfortably against the wall; Narcisa took a few steps until she was within their reach, fingered them, pointed carefully at some of the bricks, shouting as she explained the origin, the process and the completion of her creation, she gestured widely, she felt her words vibrating within her, multiplying, occupying every pore; Glorita tried to speak several times, but her voice was smothered by Narcisa's thunderous roar; she decided to leave; she had reached the door when the roar stopped her: Glorita, this is too much for you, isn't it? isn't this a fantastic creation, I know you have to get used to it, I know you have to take it in slowly, but it's all right, we'll come back so you can understand this artistic phenomenon gradually; Glorita turned around, taking advantage of a moment of silence, no, it's not too much, it's just that I don't see anything in these chimneys, I'm bored, I want to play at home; Narcisa watched her go away; she felt a growing excitement, a near exultation: Glorita had to leave because this is an artistic phenomenon and I am sure this creation is going to remain at the core of centuries; she was interrupted by a sudden jolt; she lifted up her round eyes, she looked at Don Carmelo's butterfly and heard: listen Narcisa, lower your voice, you're making so much noise you're frightening the customers; Narcisa went to the marketplace thinking that perhaps Papa was right, perhaps all Glorita wanted was to be seduced, perhaps what Glorita wanted was to stay and sleep with her; after lunch Narcisa helped Mama to her room so that she could take a nap and afterwards listen to her programs on the little radio set somebody had lent Papa at work and which she had placed on the bedside table; Narcisa went off towards her room, climbed the stairs, lay down in the bed Chebo had made; the image of Glorita invaded her closed eyes and changed into that of a nude woman with long black hair who floated in space like a nearly transparent vision; Narcisa identified a painful distance between her and the beautiful breasts and in the face that was invaded by the violence of air she recognized Margarita's childish features; Narcisa felt her fingers going over that slit that had been free of diapers for years; she kept her eyes closed, squeezing them tightly until the movement of her hand had ceased; she slept without transition; the image of the child-woman vanished and two elongated figures appeared, transparent, milky and elastic; the female figure spoke with Mama's voice; the male figure spoke with Papa's voice; they began reproaching her in unison:

you have gone over the bounds, you are beyond salvation; over and over again, every second and in eternal grief you shall read on the wall the charges and the sentence; Narcisa saw the elongated figures walk towards the wall, she saw their fingers scratching letters in the plaster; we know that one day you will bring a woman to your brother's hiding place and there you will be with her, sharing with her the same intimacy as your brother shares with his men; we know that you two have sealed this pact in the name of ancient gods; we also know about that other covenant, about that experiment that your brother has appointed for another moment of our time, when together you shall mingle the dreadful blood which is now diffused in your veins; Narcisa woke up saying no, for denying our acts is a way of saving ourselves, denying is a way of escaping punishment; but the elongated figures had disappeared and Narcisa's denial was useless, scattered on the walls of the windowless room: never have my hands touched my body or contaminated themselves in the incest of my own blood; Narcisa had no time to refute the covenants for her shouts were interrupted by Doña Flora's voice demanding from the living room: Narcisa, come and make me a cup of coffee; days followed on one another with their customary indefinite pace; months accumulated in the arnica cataplasms wrapped around Doña Flora's ankle, at the bottom of cups with a little left-over coffee, on stairs multiplied by Narcisa's shoes, in scouring pads stained with Farola, in tiles covered with wax; finally the day came when Doña

171

Flora had to start getting better, once again she had to assume the daily chores of the house, for Hilario himself had insisted before everybody: now Doña Flora, this is very strange, such a light case of synovitis shouldn't have lasted a year, there hasn't been any inflammation for some time, but if you really feel you can't move you'll have to see a specialist in Havana, for if I was unable to do anything for you then it's a case for a specialist; then Doña Flora started walking and managing everything as she had done before her accident; Narcisa returned to Cervantes, to the same grade she had interrupted the year before; once more she took up her collector's job to cover the late payments for Manengo's cinema tuition: and I'll keep paying for it for a while, my brother, until you start high school, for I've heard this course is going to be included in the program of the Institute as an additional elective, so very soon you won't have to pay anything and I'll be able to leave the job; Narcisa remembered her brother's silence, the mouth pursed in a little circle giving a shape to his reproach: and are you so silly as to think I won't have any expenses? do you think I can carry on and not buy even the most elementary equipment? Narcisa watched him go away without breaking the silence that had suddenly opened before her; Narcisa kept on with her collecting schedule without having much time to think that during this year, 1952, everybody had by now forgotten the first bomb at Pearl Harbor and the occasional queues in front of the bakeries which, according to public rumor, were the result of the

172

scarcity of flour; on Sunday the monotonous daily rhythm was interrupted by an excursion to Duaba Beach; Mama had been feeling ill since the day before, her chest was congested, she had a little flu and a fever of thirty-seven and a half and she insisted, well, this isn't really fever, it's nothing serious and we are not going to miss the beach just for that, it's not every day Pascual decides to take us out of the house; Sunday was cloudy, with brief and intermittent showers; when they returned home Narcisa went to the emergency pharmacy to consult Hilario: listen Hilario, Mama has a fever of thirty-eight and a half, she feels ill, her chest is congested...; Hilario gave a prescription right away: antiphlogistine cataplasms, sulfa powder; more powder to get the temperature down; that night Don Pascual had to sleep on the sofa, for with the moaning and all the medicine Narcisa had to give to his wife he would not have been able to sleep a wink; Narcisa prepared to spend the night in a rocking chair next to Mama; she had already applied the cataplasm and administered some sulfa powder; according to Hilario's instructions she would have to wait three hours until the next medicine; night was drawing on, the fever had gone up; Mama was drowsy and slept restlessly, vainly seeking a comfortable position for her body; in the semi-darkness Narcisa watched her restless gestures alternating with sentences that spilled out with difficulty, like a litany: I am the thick-lipped tick of the district of Juana Luz; I humbly confess that the wings of my nose are like patent leather; it's the uterine fire of mollusks and

173

soldiers; I am the desperate mouse hanging on to
birthday candles; I am the incandescent little tail of
iguanas from the Galapagos; those hypocrites that put
their tails in birthday candles should be hanged in
Trafalgar; Doña Flora sat up; Narcisa tried to calm her
as she could, battling against her insistence: I must go to
the multifarious senatorial street; when daylight broke
Doña Flora was quieter: I feel as if I came out of a long
and distant dream that took me to a world full of
absurdities; Narcisa made sure that her mother would
not worry unnecessarily: it's all right Mama, you
expressed yourself in a multiple language that can be
understood in more than four tensions; Doña Flora
looked at her daughter and she thought, not even now
that she's twelve years old and menstruating is it
possible to understand her or to say anything to her, but
now, what can you expect, when she became a woman
she wasn't even aware of it, she didn't know what it was
all about when it started a few months ago, Pascual told
me everything, Narcisa is sitting on the doorstep and
she sees all that blood on her skirt and she runs out to
the street till she sees Pascual walking on the sidewalk
near the house; Papa, Papa, look what happened to me,
this is the signal of my death, look, I've swallowed
something that has cut me all up inside, tell me Papa,
am I bleeding to death? just imagine her coming to
Pascual with this story, so Pascual had to tell her, this is
women's business, you'll have to speak with your
mother; and there goes Narcisa insisting, Mama knows
nothing about anything, it's you who reads, it's you who

174

has read *Les Misérables* and who knows the most in our family; and Pascual had to grab her by the hand and bring her to me and just imagine her saying I don't know anything when I explained it all to her, look Narcisa, this is women's business and this is going to happen to you for many years and the only thing you can do is wear this piece of antiseptic cloth so you won't get dirty and when this one is full, well, you wash it and you put on a clean one and from now on you are in danger of men getting you pregnant, so don't you go near a man if you don't want to end up with a swollen belly; during all these months Narcisa had followed Doña Flora's instructions, feeling a little terrified when she came near men; if a man touches me I could become pregnant and I must be especially careful about Manengo's urine because I could get a swollen belly, so each time I have to use the toilet I wash the edge of the seat with a can of water before I sit down, for how awful if Manengo gave me a swollen belly; Doña Flora got up without help and Narcisa asked for permission to go and lie down a little for she had not slept all night; in her room she took off her shoes, lay down on her bed, covered herself with the sheet, closed her eyes and prepared to go to sleep; she felt the bed changing into a crib, she felt her body becoming smaller and more remote in time and space, she went back to the Marsh of Zapata, swiftly she went back to a bed in a house in a street in Baracoa where her mother's womb was waiting for her; she traveled blindly through the womb, she regressed further, to a space where she did not yet

175

possess a shape; she knew that the other shapeless thing floating in the air at her side was Manengo; she understood that he was saying to her: you and I will be brother and sister on earth and this makes no difference to me, for my fate is to be a star whose light you can never dim, not even with the slightest part of your shadow; your destiny is to reflect my light; it is your destiny that all shall be condemned to forget your name; it is your destiny that others will only take notice of you when they recognize in you the kindred of my blood; but as for those two who are going to be my parents, I did not choose them for this life and from now on I shall let them feel the weight of my rebellion; when Narcisa opened her eyes she remembered what her mother had told her so many times: while I was expecting Manengo terrible things were happening in this house, horses trotted around and came to demolish everything, they came to destroy us, I heard the sound of chains striking the walls; pots jumped out of the shelves from their appointed places in the cupboards and crashed to the floor and I did tell Pascual, listen Pascual, what are we bringing into the world? Narcisa got up and decided to keep Mama company, once and for all she would communicate with her; she found her in the kitchen, making herself a cup of linden tea which she took to drink at the table in the living room; Narcisa sat down by her side: Mama, what about Mulata Road, do you think it's really going to be built? it's going to be a fantastic road Mama, because it's going to go from Baracoa and cross the whole Toa Valley and reach as

176

far as Santiago de Cuba; Doña Flora was looking vacantly at a point on the tablecloth: Narcisa, the only thing I can tell you is that with so many expenses and with Pascual's salary as it is I haven't been to the Encanto Cinema for ages, I've missed *The Third Man* and now *Arch of Triumph* is coming and I don't know where we'll get the money and even when I've already seen a movie I like to see it again, the only one who never misses a movie is Manengo, but we can't depend on him to even tell us what the films are about, he just says we wouldn't understand and that's it; Narcisa checked the facts with Papa, for he was the one who really knew about all those things: Mulata Road would go through el Manguito and la Maya and not through Cueto and San Luis; night took Narcisa back to her bed, which began to change into a crib with a magic speed that could not be measured in time; Narcisa felt her skin shrinking at the blow of these words: "your destiny is to reflect my light; it is your destiny that all shall be condemned to forget your name"; then she recalled that two weeks ago her shoes had started taking her assiduously to the workshop; she let her memory repeat the ritual she had performed every day, at the exact instant of sunset: she increased her height by standing on a brick pedestal, spread out her arms, leaned her head back as if to let her chin receive the last beams of the sun: "from here, by the conjuration of the tensions of the gods, on this wheel on which it is our destiny to revolve I decree that when the equinox places the sun on the semi-rhomboidal steps that occupy the back of the rattle snake, the triumph and the greatness of my work shall be proclaimed with a clap of thunder at the center of the pyramid; the light of my work shall dim yours and you shall reflect my light"; after two weeks of repeating this ritual, Narcisa had almost achieved serenity and the astonishment in her eyes had changed into a capacity for self-love; this mood was only broken on the last day by the alarm caused by the fleeting presence of her brother, whom she recognized hastening out of the door of the workshop and she heard the voice again, which today shattered her with: *your destiny is to reflect my light; it is your destiny that all shall be condemned to forget your name*; this had brought back her astonishment, this had made her defenseless against the process that made her body shrink inexorably; she sensed that the diaper covering the small slit was heavy with urine and clung to the rash on the plump, swollen and irritated lips; the air was filled with instants which had been dislocated from the akasic records and which surrounded the crib; she knew it would be some time yet before the promise she had made to herself while she lay on her back in the wet mud of the Marsh would be fulfilled: her voice would soar into space and propagate that message she had carried with her in the center of her forehead for so many centuries and which would amaze the world: "Republic, Republic, Plato, Aristotle and don't forget Socrates, Krishna, Krishna, Krishna"; while she remembered the promise other moments invaded her consciousness: Pascual, Pascual, where on earth did that boy go? Pascual, Pascual, what shall we name this one? it's nothing lady, it stinks, it stinks like rotten eggs and the sea is getting black over there, it's all from that dead thing, that dead animal with a swollen belly you see floating over there; there's nothing I can do Flora, this one won't go away so easily, you can be sure she'll be back on her own and in a minute she'll be back here with us; alright Pascual, let's turn back, now that everything is settled, all I want to do is get home quickly and change because this bundle's got me all soaked; Narcisa lay in her crib, attentive and motionless, once again she became conscious of her own breathing; her open eyes were fixed on the wall and made out the traits of a monster in the lines of ink forming a picture there; next to it there was another set of dense black lines outlining another monster; on the other side, another and another still, four of them lined up in a row; the monstrous harrowed faces started going round the crib and asked her to account for her actions; Narcisa felt a fluttering in her chest, an urge to justify herself so that everyone would know that she was not guilty of anything, that everything had an explanation; she stood up in the crib, she kept looking at the faces that insisted on her accounting for her actions; Narcisa felt terror invading her, she did not know how to overpower them, suddenly, with a gesture that surprised even herself, she spread out her right hand as if trying to communicate with them; the monsters went on scrutinizing her; Narcisa heard herself saying, lovely, you are all lovely, lovely faces; the monsters wheeled around slowly and turned their back on her and Narcisa

179

understood the command without hearing it, she felt her astral body gliding through the air and following the monsters who embedded themselves in the wall once more; she felt them urging her with their non-existent fingers, ordering her to place herself on the empty canvas that was waiting for her; then she felt the rigidity of the black lines forming her face; she felt the absolute immobility of her expression; after going through a period of incubation she opened her eyes and from the picture she occupied she now began to see everything clearly; she was aware that three years had passed since her last ritual in the workshop and that all calendars now indicated the year 1955; she recognized Tenth of October Street; she recognized the door of her house; one by one she recognized the four figures; she recognized herself, she had grown a great deal, she was almost a woman; she saw Manengo preparing for the premiere of his first film, a student project that had earned him a scholarship to Rome; she saw Papa's and Mama's popularity growing, they were the parents of a son who would travel abroad; she heard Mama engrossed in conversation with her friend Pancha: you see Pancha, that's what I always said about my son, he's got talent I'm telling you and now he's going all the way to *Chinechitá*, that's what they call that place where all those movie directors live and he'll be in that *Chinechitá* with all of them, just imagine, I'm in such a hurry to set my curlers and get my hair done, today there's going to be a show of my son's first movie at the Institute, he directed it and even wrote it himself, well, you know, the film only lasts a few minutes but Manengo is only seventeen and he's got a scholarship to go to Europe and if you knew the fright this gave me because when I first heard about it I thought he was going to China till somebody explained everything to me about that *Chinechitá*, that's where movie directors live in Rome, it must be a kind of big house like a boarding house or barracks, alright Pancha, I keep talking and I'm not setting my hair, so now you know, at the Institute at seven tonight, Manengo says the first row is reserved for us so we can see everything up close; from the rigidity of the black lines Narcisa could see herself as she had always been; she was made of that mass of cells and blood which had coated her bones when she had started to occupy her place in the womb; she knew that she had turned fifteen a few weeks before and that there had not been any party and as a late gift she had been given a new cotton dress to wear at the premiere of her brother's film; at six-thirty all five members of the family walked to the Institute; after a few minutes the theater darkened and the title could be seen clearly: *THE DOGS IN THE PUDDLE*, subtitled *Magical Realism in Five Voices* and in the lower right corner, *A FILM by Manén*; the silence was broken by Doña Flora's protest directed at her husband: what's all this about Manén, why does Manengo reject his Christian name of Pascual, Jr. and what about your last name and mine? her words were silenced by Pascual's "Flora, be quiet," but at the same time he was thinking that his son would never change, this business about Manén was not a manly thing to do and it's unmanly to reject one's father's name; the dedication of the film made him more uneasy: "to my mother, who never understood my love for the cinema; to my father, who never understood me"; Don Pascual felt ashamed anticipating the comments he would have to bear at the Health Department and Doña Flora was already preparing a reply to Pancha's remarks: saying I don't understand his love for the cinema and one day I wanted to discuss *Spellbound* with him and he was the one who didn't want to sit down and talk about it, but I let this pass because people who've got so much talent are like that sometimes; Doña Flora's attention returned to the screen where she saw five dogs around a street puddle, their snouts flat in the muddy water; they looked as if they were seeking their reflections there; each member of the family gradually recognized himself in one of the canine characters; Narcisa understood that she was that mixture of bull-dog and Pekingese with thin mangy hair; Florita-Ita recognized herself in the poodle with the perfectly groomed coat; Doña Flora identified herself as the fat mongrel bitch with hanging teats, lumbering, and with whitish, slightly curly hair; Don Pascual identified himself as the short-haired mongrel, black with yellow streaks and piercing gaze; everyone understood that Manengo had chosen to be the Great Dane, in whose graceful arrogance Pascual detected a feminine fragility; after a few seconds during which the dogs look intensely into the puddle, their expressions change, they become fierce, their lips curl up and reveal

182

a tight and terrifying array of teeth and fangs; the dog representing Narcisa barks loudly, the others surround her so that she has to walk into the puddle, they make her stand in the middle; the dogs place themselves in cross formation, each occupying one of the four cardinal points; slowly they come near the center where the barking continues; a close-up of the four dogs enlarges on the screen, the rigid jaws open; the four dogs tighten the circle and finally the bark changes to a brief howl; simultaneously with the words *THE END*, Narcisa's applause and her words of enthusiasm burst out: my brother, what a beautiful film, what lovely harmony in our family, this is why I love you all so much, because of the perfection exhaled by our holiness; her glistening round eyes met her brother's severe glance: Narcisa, we always suspected it, you cannot love us unless you invent us, unless you make us into something we are not; this horrible thing you saw in the film, this is our reality, this is the cement that unites our clan beyond all hatred and all rejection; you have no right to make us disappear, you cannot and shall not rob us of our essence and transform us into visions of your mind which have nothing to do with us; the friends and neighbors who had seen the film surrounded Papa and Mama to congratulate them on the talent of their son whom they now regarded with awed respect; Manengo decided when it was time to leave; he walked along the hallway, followed by Mama, Papa and his sisters; on the way home Narcisa felt that the group headed by Manengo was moving away from her, as though the

183

four of them had decided they wanted to ignore her; Manengo's key opened the door; in the living room Narcisa understood the wordless command and went up to her room; she hung her new dress in the wardrobe, took off her shoes, put on a long white flannel gown, moved her bed to the center of the room, lay down on her back, her arms crossed on her chest; through the door opening she heard the four coming in, led by Manengo, each moved like an automaton to a corner of the room; Narcisa's body was covered in cold sweat, the others' gaze fell upon it; she felt their power over her, she wanted to flee, to be changed into the *tibaracón*; she wanted to be the torrential rain of the jungle, she wanted to be the eternally flowing river that joins with the ocean; to be river, movement, to flow, to flow, but a sudden jolt, and everything became dark; the gazes from the four corners of the room remained fixed on Narcisa for a long time until her body was completely inert; a glance from Manengo in his corner transmitted the information to the figures in the other three corners; that glance also gave them the order to leave and, led by Manengo, they all filed silently out the door; the black lines forming Narcisa's face in the picture gradually disappear, the only thing that remains is a pair of round eyes, witnesses to the last supper: on the table, Narcisa's naked corpse; at each end, Papa and Manengo in formal attire; Mama and Florita-Ita, elegantly dressed, facing each other between the two men; Manengo authorizes the first cut, initiated by Papa; with the huge knife in his hand he firmly cuts a long thin slice from one of the legs and places it on his plate; the blade shines in Florita-Ita's hands, she slices pieces from the hip with ease; Mama's turn is interrupted by a protest: but what's this jet of blood that's soiling my dress? is blood still supposed to come out of the liver? before he starts cutting Manengo closes his sister's eyes delicately, almost tenderly; he then makes a cut from the elbow to the shoulder; he deftly places the slice on his spotless plate; with cider he proposes a toast to the success of *The Dogs in the Puddle*; then an unexpected thought overcomes him: what shall we do with the left-overs? Don Pascual's voice wastes no time in replying: this is for the funeral... for the funeral we'll have to celebrate for everyone

Glossary of Cuban Terms

azabache: jetstone. A jetstone amulet was pinned to a baby's clothes to ward off the evil eye if the child was praised for its beauty.

bacán: typical Cuban dish originating in Baracoa.

café con leche: coffee with milk (2/3 milk, 1/3 espresso coffee), the most common breakfast drink.

cantina: aluminum container for a ready-made meal. These containers were placed one above the other and used to carry cooked food, usually sold and distributed by individual families.

cocido: Cuban dish of chickpeas, Spanish sausage, potatoes and cabbage.

cucurucho: Cuban sweet. A conical container made from plantain leaves is filled with a mixture of grated coconut cooked in molasses or brown sugar.

danzón: typical Cuban dance with a slow rhythm played by a flute.

flauta (flute) of bread: loaf of bread about one yard long and three inches wide.

guineos or *plátanos manzanos*: bananas. The first term is used in the province of Oriente where Baracoa is located, the second in the city and province of Havana.

Materva: soft drink made with *yerba mate* or Paraguay tea, a South American species of holly.

medio: coin equivalent to five cents of a Cuban peso.

mojo: dressing made with oil, vinegar, salt, lemon and garlic.

nansú: delicate cotton fabric.

peso: Cuban currency equivalent to one U.S. dollar at the time.

quilo or *centavo*: coin equivalent to one cent of a Cuban peso.

real: coin equivalent to ten cents of a Cuban peso.

tibaracón: a geographical phenomenon of the region of Baracoa due to the strong waves which prevent rivers from flowing directly into the sea. Sand and sediment accumulate, forming a barrier which forces rivers to run parallel to the sea until they can disembogue. This phenomenon occurs at the mouth of the Macaguanigua and Miel rivers, among others.

twelve grapes: While the bells ring at midnight on the 31st of December, it is the custom in Cuba to eat twelve grapes to bring luck during the forthcoming twelve months.

vianda: starchy vegetables, including sweet potatoes, yams, plantains, cassava, arum etc.

About the Author: Mireya Robles was born in Cuba in 1934 and studied civil and international law at the University of Havana. In 1957 she left for the United States, where she earned a doctorate in Hispanic Studies at the State University of New York.

Two volumes of her poetry have been published in Spain and Mexico in 1973 and 1976. Other poems have appeared in Italian, French and English translation. Her poetry, stories and essays have also featured in three Spanish-language anthologies published in New York. In 1971 Mireya Robles won the first Iberoamerican Poets' Prize in New York. In 1974 she won the gold medal for poetry given by the French Academie Internationale de Lutèce.

From its first publication in Spanish in 1985, Robles' novel *Hagiography of Narcisa the Beautiful* has proved a critically important text in Hispanic and Women's Studies. The author has also written other novels, *La muerte definitiva de Pedro el Largo* (*The Definitive Death of Peter the Long*) and *Una mujer y otras cuatro* (*One Woman and Another Four*), runner-up for the *Premio Nadal* in Spain, and *Combinado del Este*.

From 1985-1994 she was a Lecturer in Hispanic Studies at the University of Natal in Durban, South Africa, and she is currently a Research Associate at that university.